James Schoolcraft Sherman (late vice president of the United States) Memorial addresses delivered at a joint session of the Senate and the House of Representatives of the United States February 15, 1913 and an account of the funeral services in Utica, N.Y

United States. Congress (62nd, 3rd session : 1912-1913)

JAMES SCHOOLCRAFT SHERMAN

# JAMES SCHOOLCRAFT SHERMAN

(Late Vice President of the United States)

## MEMORIAL ADDRESSES

DELIVERED AT A JOINT SESSION OF THE SENATE
AND THE HOUSE OF REPRESENTATIVES
OF THE UNITED STATES
FEBRUARY 15, 1913

AND

AN ACCOUNT OF THE FUNERAL SERVICES
IN UTICA, N. Y., NOVEMBER 2, 1912

---

PREPARED UNDER THE DIRECTION OF
THE JOINT COMMITTEE ON PRINTING

WASHINGTON
GOVERNMENT PRINTING OFFICE
1913

*B4354*

## S CON. RES No 41, 62D CONGRESS.

[Passed Mar 1 (calendar day, Mar 2), 1913 ]

*Resolved by the Senate (the House of Representatives concurring)*, That there shall be printed and bound, under the direction of the Joint Committee on Printing, fourteen thousand one hundred copies of the proceedings and the eulogies delivered in Congress on James Schoolcraft Sherman, late Vice President of the United States, with illustration, of which four thousand copies shall be for the use of the Senate, eight thousand copies for the use of the House of Representatives, two thousand copies for the use of the Senators and Representatives of the State of New York, and one hundred copies, bound in full morocco, for the use of Mrs. James Schoolcraft Sherman· *Provided*, That there shall be included in such publication the proclamation of the President and the proceedings in the Supreme Court of the United States upon the death of Vice President Sherman, and an account of the funeral services at Utica, New York

Attest:

                                     CHARLES G BENNETT,
                                     *Secretary of the Senate*

Attest:

                                     SOUTH TRIMBLE,
                     *Clerk of the House of Representatives*

# CONTENTS

# BIOGRAPHY

[Revised from last biographical sketch approved by Mr SHERMAN for insertion in the April, 1912, edition of the Congressional Directory, second session of the Sixty-second Congress ]

JAMES SCHOOLCRAFT SHERMAN, of Utica, N Y., Vice President of the United States from March 4, 1909, to October 30, 1912, was born in the city of Utica October 24, 1855, his father, Richard U. Sherman, also born in Oneida County, N. Y., was by profession an editor and also prominent in public life. The son was graduated from Hamilton College in 1878, was a lawyer by profession, but retired from practice in 1906, was married in 1881 to Carrie Babcock, at East Orange, N. J ; three sons—Sherrill, Richard U., and Thomas M—are living and in business at Utica, was president of the Utica Trust & Deposit Co., of Utica, N. Y, and an officer and director of various local business enterprises, was an attendant of the Dutch Reformed Church and chairman of its board of trustees, a graduate of Hamilton College, which college, as well as Wesleyan University and Pittsburgh University, conferred upon him the degree of LL D. He was a member of the Royal Arcanum and the Order of Elks. He was also a member of all the local clubs at Utica, of the Union League, Republican, and Transportation Clubs, of New York City, of the Metropolitan, University, Chevy Chase, and Columbia Clubs, of Washington. He had been active in Republican politics since 1879; was a frequent delegate to State conventions, and presided over the New York State Republican conventions in 1895, 1900, and 1908, was delegate to the Republican national convention of 1892, vice chairman of the Republican national congressional committee for many years prior to 1906, in which year he was chairman of the committee. He appeared upon the platform in various States in every campaign from 1892 down to the year of his death, was mayor of Utica in 1884 and a Member of Congress continuously from 1886 to 1908, with a two-year interim from 1890 to 1892. While in Congress he served on the Committees on the Judiciary, the Census, Industrial Arts and Expositions, Interstate and Foreign Commerce, Rules, and Indian Affairs, of which latter committee he was chairman for 14 years, was elected Vice President upon the ticket with President Taft in 1908 for the term which ended March 4, 1913 Renominated for Vice President by the Republican convention in 1912 His last public speech (Senate Doc 943, 62d Cong.) was made in Utica, August 21, 1912, when he again accepted a place on the Republican ticket with President Taft. Died in Utica, N. Y., October 30, 1912, and was buried in Forest Hill Cemetery, Utica, November 2, 1912.

# DEATH OF HON. JAMES SCHOOLCRAFT SHERMAN

## PROCEEDINGS IN THE SENATE

MONDAY, *December 2, 1912.*

The first Monday in December being the day prescribed by the Constitution of the United States for the annual meeting of Congress, the third session of the Sixty-second Congress commenced on this day

The Senate assembled in its Chamber at the Capitol.

Augustus O. Bacon, a Senator from the State of Georgia, took the chair as President pro tempore under the order of the Senate of August 17, 1912.

The President pro tempore called the Senate to order at 12 o'clock noon.

The Chaplain, Rev. Ulysses G. B. Pierce, D. D., offered the following prayer:

Almighty God, our heavenly Father, in whose presence we now stand, we are come together in Thy name and to do Thy will. At the opening of this session of Congress we invoke Thy blessing. Without Thee we can do nothing. Until Thou dost bless us, our highest wisdom is but folly and our utmost strength but utter weakness. Bestow upon us, therefore, we humbly pray Thee, wisdom and strength from above, that so we may glorify Thee, accomplishing that which Thou givest us to do.

We come before Thee, our Father, with a deepened sense of our dependence upon Thee. Thou hast made us to know how frail we are. Thou hast showed us that the

[7]

way of man is not in himself alone, and that it is not in us who walk to direct our steps. Thou hast called from his earthly labors Thy servant, the Vice President of our Nation. While we thought it was still day Thou didst cause the sun of his life to go down, bringing the night, when no man can work We murmur not nor repine, our Father, knowing that alike the day and the night are Thine. Thou hast taken from our side fellow laborers and companions, leaving in this Senate empty seats and in our hearts loneliness and sorrow. We can not forget them, our Father, though in the flesh we behold their faces no more Thou hast removed from his post of duty an officer of this body and has made us to know that in the midst of life we are in death. Comfort our hearts, we beseech Thee, for all our sorrows, and keep us evermore in Thy love; and though Thou feed us with the bread of adversity and give us to drink of the water of affliction, yet take not from us Thy holy spirit.

We pray Thee to bless the President of the United States. Uphold him by Thy power, watch over him by Thy providence, guide him by Thy wisdom, and strengthen him with Thy heavenly grace. Bless him who shall preside over this Senate, bestowing upon him all things as shall seem good unto Thee. For all who are in authority we pray that they may serve Thee with singleness of purpose, for the good of this people and for Thy glory.

So, our Father, may this session of Congress, begun in Thy name, be continued in Thy fear and ended in Thine honor. Grant us so to labor that by our deliberations we may hasten the time when Thy kingdom shall come and Thy will shall be done on earth as it is in heaven.

In the name which is above every name, hear our prayer. Amen.

### DEATH OF THE VICE PRESIDENT

Mr. ROOT. Mr. President, with a deep sense of public loss and of personal bereavement I discharge the duty of announcing to the Senate that on the 30th day of October last, at his home in the city of Utica, JAMES SCHOOL-CRAFT SHERMAN, the Vice President of the United States, departed this life.

His serene and cheerful temperament, inspired by love of country and of his kind, will no more diffuse through this body a sense of reasonableness, of friendliness, and of kindly consideration  His faculty of swift and just decision which has promoted and cleared the path of public business in the Senate for the three years which are past will no longer aid us in our deliberations.

I have the honor to offer the resolutions which I now send to the desk.

The resolutions (S. Res. 390) were read, considered by unanimous consent, and unanimously agreed to, as follows:

*Resolved,* That the Senate has heard with profound sorrow and regret the announcement of the death of JAMES SCHOOLCRAFT SHERMAN, late Vice President of the United States.

*Resolved,* That the Secretary communicate these resolutions to the House of Representatives and transmit a copy thereof to the family of the deceased.

The PRESIDENT pro tempore. In connection with the announcement just made the Chair now lays before the Senate a cablegram received from the Brazilian Senate and the reply thereto, in order that the same may now be read and become a part of the Record, and to be on a later day given such disposition as the Senate may direct.

The matter entire is as follows.

RIO DE JANEIRO, VIA DAKAR,
*Noviembre 6, 1912.*

Sr. PRESIDENTE SENADO,
*Senate, Washington*

Cumpro dever communicar V ex que Senado Brasil sentido vivamente morte eminente Sr. JAMES SHERMAN, Vice Presidente dessa grande Republica, deliberou inserir acta seus trabalhos voto profundo pezar por esse doloroso acontecimento, e transmittir Senado Americano sinceras condoleancias, o que em seu nome faco por intermedio V. ex. a quem apresento minhas attenciosas saudacoes.

FERREIRA CHAVES,
*1º Secretario do Senado.*

[Translation of cablegram ]

RIO DE JANEIRO, VIA DAKAR,
*November 6, 1912.*

PRESIDENT OF THE SENATE,
*Washington·*

I perform the duty of informing Your Excellency that the Senate of Brazil, keenly afflicted by the death of the eminent Mr. JAMES SHERMAN, Vice President of your great Republic, has voted to enter upon its journal a resolution of profound sympathy in that sorrowful event and to transmit to the American Senate sincere condolence, which I do in its name through Your Excellency, to whom I present my respectful salutations

FERREIRA CHAVES,
*First Secretary of the Senate.*

[Cablegram.]

WASHINGTON, *November 7, 1912.*

To the PRESIDENT OF THE BRAZILIAN SENATE·

I have received your very considerate and cordial message of sympathy, addressed to the American Senate, on the occasion of the death of the late Vice President JAMES SHERMAN.

The Senate of the United States is not now in session. So soon as it convenes in December I will have the honor to lay before that body your highly esteemed message. I beg, in the meantime, to thank your honorable body for its kindly consideration and sympathy.

AUGUSTUS O. BACON,
*President of the Senate pro tempore.*

[NOTE—The foregoing reply to the cablegram of the Brazilian Senate was, upon the request of Senator Bacon, cabled to the American ambassador at Brazil by the Acting Secretary of State, with directions for immediate delivery.]

Mr CULLOM. Mr. President, I desire as a further mark of respect to offer the following resolution, and I ask for its present consideration.

The resolution (S. Res. 393) was read, considered by unanimous consent, and unanimously agreed to, as follows:

*Resolved,* That as a further mark of respect to the memory of the late Vice President JAMES SCHOOLCRAFT SHERMAN and the late Senators Weldon Brinton Heyburn and Isidor Rayner, whose deaths have just been announced, the Senate do now adjourn

Thereupon the Senate (at 12 o'clock and 22 minutes p. m.) adjourned until to-morrow, Tuesday, December 3, 1912, at 11 o'clock a. m.

WEDNESDAY, *December 4, 1912.*

Mr. POINDEXTER. Mr. President, I present a series of resolutions adopted by the people of the city of Olympia, State of Washington, in commemoration of the late Vice President I ask that the resolutions may lie on the table and be printed in the Record

By unanimous consent, the resolutions were ordered to lie on the table and to be printed in the Record, as follows:

Whereas death has removed from his earthly labors the Hon JAMES SCHOOLCRAFT SHERMAN, late Vice President of the United States, and

Whereas we realize that he represented the highest type of American manhood, and that by his unwavering devotion to duty as he saw it he deserved well of his country and the world: Now therefore be it

*Resolved by the people of the city of Olympia, Wash, and vicinity, assembled without regard to political affiliations or*

*beliefs,* That we deplore the untimely death of Hon. JAMES SCHOOLCRAFT SHERMAN and deeply feel the loss that our Nation has sustained, and that we extend to his stricken family the heartfelt sympathy of this community; be it further

*Resolved,* That the chairman of this meeting, over his signature, transmit a copy of these resolutions to the widow of our lamented Vice President, a copy to the President of the United States, and a copy to the Senators from the State of Washington, to be presented to the Senate of the United States.

The foregoing resolution was unanimously passed at an assemblage of the citizens of Olympia, Wash., held in the Capital Park on Saturday, November 2, 1912.

CHAS D. KING, *Chairman.*

FRIDAY, *December 13, 1912.*

Mr. Root submitted the following resolution (S. Res. 408), which was read, considered by unanimous consent, and unanimously agreed to:

*Resolved,* That the Senate of the United States acknowledges with grateful appreciation the sympathy of the Senate of Brazil in the loss suffered by the American Government and people in the lamented death of Vice President SHERMAN, and it begs the Senate of Brazil to accept the assurance of its most respectful consideration and friendship.

The Secretary is directed to transmit a copy of this resolution to the first secretary of the Senate of Brazil.

SATURDAY, *January 11, 1913.*

Mr. Root submitted the following resolution (S. Res. 426), which was read, considered by unanimous consent, and agreed to:

*Resolved,* That the Committee on Rules be, and it is, directed to report to the Senate an order for suitable ceremonies in the Senate in honor of the memory of the late Vice President of the United States, JAMES S. SHERMAN.

SATURDAY, *January 18, 1913.*

Mr. CUMMINS. From the Committee on Rules, to which was referred Senate resolution 426, directing the Committee on Rules to report an order for ceremonies in honor of the memory of the late Vice President JAMES S. SHERMAN, I report a resolution which I ask to have read and referred to the Committee to Audit and Control the Contingent Expenses of the Senate.

The resolution (S. Res. 435) was read and referred to the Committee to Audit and Control the Contingent Expenses of the Senate, as follows

*Resolved*, That Saturday, the 15th day of February, be set apart for appropriate exercises in commemoration of the life, character, and public service of the late JAMES S SHERMAN, Vice President of the United States and President of the Senate of the United States.

That a committee of three Senators, composed of Elihu Root, James O'Gorman, and Charles Curtis, is hereby appointed with full power to make all arrangements and publish a suitable program for the aforesaid meeting of the Senate and to issue the invitations hereinafter mentioned

That invitations shall be extended to the President of the United States, the members of the Cabinet, the Chief Justice and Justices of the Supreme Court, the Speaker and Members of the House of Representatives, the judges of the Commerce Court, the judges of the Court of Customs Appeals, the judges of the courts of the District of Columbia, the officers of the Army and Navy stationed in Washington, the members of the Interstate Commerce Commission, the members of the Civil Service Commission. That such other invitations shall be issued as to the said committee shall seem best.

All expenses incurred by the committee in the execution of this order shall be paid from the contingent fund of the Senate.

MONDAY, *January 27, 1913.*

Mr. Briggs, from the Committee to Audit and Control the Contingent Expenses of the Senate, to which was referred Senate resolution No. 435, setting apart a day for appropriate exercises in commemoration of the life, character, and public services of the late Vice President, submitted by Mr. Cummins on the 18th instant, reported it without amendment

TUESDAY, *January 28, 1913.*

Mr CUMMINS. I ask unanimous consent for the present consideration of Senate resolution 435, a resolution submitted by me and reported yesterday from the Committee to Audit and Control the Contingent Expenses of the Senate by the Senator from New Jersey [Mr. Briggs].

There being no objection, the resolution was considered and agreed to, as follows.

*Resolved,* That Saturday, the 15th day of February, be set apart for appropriate exercises in commemoration of the life, character, and public service of the late JAMES S. SHERMAN, Vice President of the United States and President of the Senate of the United States.

That a committee of three Senators, composed of Elihu Root, James A. O'Gorman, and Charles Curtis, is hereby appointed, with full power to make all arrangements and publish a suitable program for the aforesaid meeting of the Senate, and to issue the invitations hereinafter mentioned.

That invitations shall be extended to the President of the United States, the members of the Cabinet, the Chief Justice and Justices of the Supreme Court, the Speaker and Members of the House of Representatives, the judges of the Commerce Court, the judges of the Court of Customs Appeals, the judges of the courts of the District of Columbia, the officers of the Army and Navy stationed in Washington, the members of the Interstate Commerce Commission, and the members of the Civil Service Commission That such other invitations shall be issued as to the said committee shall seem best.

All expenses incurred by the committee in the execution of this order shall be paid from the contingent fund of the Senate.

WEDNESDAY, *February 5, 1913.*

Mr. Root submitted the following resolution (S. Res. 451), which was read, considered by unanimous consent, and agreed to

*Resolved,* That the Senate extend to the Speaker and the Members of the House of Representatives an invitation to attend the exercises in commemoration of the life, character, and public services of the late JAMES S. SHERMAN, Vice President of the

United States and President of the Senate, to be held in the Senate Chamber on Saturday, the 15th day of February next at 12 o'clock noon.

FRIDAY, *February 7, 1913*

A message from the House of Representatives, by J. C. South, its Chief Clerk, announced that the House accepts the invitation of the Senate extended to the Speaker and Members of the House of Representatives to attend the exercises in commemoration of the life, character, and public services of the late JAMES S. SHERMAN, Vice President of the United States and President of the Senate, to be held in the Senate Chamber on Saturday, the 15th day of February next, at 12 o'clock noon.

[INVITATION]

The Senate of the United States
requests your presence at the
Ceremonies in honor of the memory
of the late
James Schoolcraft Sherman,
Vice President of the United States,
to be held in the Senate Chamber,
on Saturday, the 15th of February, 1913,
at twelve o'clock noon.

[PROGRAM]

*Memorial Ceremonies*
*in honor of the late*

*James Schoolcraft Sherman,*

*Vice President of the United States,*

*February 15th, 1913.*

## ORDER OF EXERCISES

———

PRESIDENT PRO TEMPORE CALLS THE SENATE TO ORDER AT 12 O'CLOCK NOON

PRESIDENT DIRECTS THE SECRETARY TO READ, AND THE SECRETARY READS THE FOLLOWING RESOLUTION GOVERNING THE PROCEEDINGS OF THE DAY

RESOLVED, THAT SATURDAY, THE 15TH DAY OF FEBRUARY, BE SET APART FOR APPROPRIATE EXERCISES IN COMMEMORATION OF THE LIFE, CHARACTER, AND PUBLIC SERVICE OF THE LATE JAMES S SHERMAN VICE PRESIDENT OF THE UNITED STATES AND PRESIDENT OF THE SENATE OF THE UNITED STATES

SERGEANT AT ARMS ANNOUNCES THE SPEAKER AND MEMBERS OF THE HOUSE OF REPRESENTATIVES

SERGEANT AT ARMS ANNOUNCES THE CHIEF JUSTICE AND ASSOCIATE JUSTICES OF THE SUPREME COURT OF THE UNITED STATES

SERGEANT AT ARMS ANNOUNCES THE AMBASSADORS AND MINISTERS PLENIPOTENTIARY TO THE UNITED STATES

SERGEANT AT ARMS ANNOUNCES THE PRESIDENT OF THE UNITED STATES AND MEMBERS OF HIS CABINET

ALL HAVING BEEN SEATED, THE CEREMONIES OF THIS OCCA-
SION WILL BE OPENED BY PRAYER BY THE CHAPLAIN OF
THE SENATE

THE PRESIDENT OF THE SENATE RECOGNIZES THE SENATORS
WHO ARE TO SPEAK IN THE FOLLOWING ORDER

> MR ROOT
> MR MARTIN
> MR GALLINGER
> MR THORNTON
> MR. LODGE
> MR KERN
> MR LA FOLLETTE
> MR WILLIAMS
> MR CURTIS
> MR CUMMINS
> MR OLIVER
> MR O'GORMAN

THE PRESIDENT OF THE SENATE RECOGNIZES THE SPEAKER OF
THE HOUSE OF REPRESENTATIVES

THE PRESIDENT OF THE SENATE RECOGNIZES THE PRESIDENT
OF THE UNITED STATES.

THE PRESIDENT OF THE SENATE RECOGNIZES SENATOR ROOT,
WHO MOVES ADJOURNMENT

# MEMORIAL EXERCISES

SATURDAY, *February 15, 1913.*

*(Legislative day of Tuesday, February 11, 1913.)*

The Senate reassembled at 12 o'clock meridian, on the expiration of the recess.

The President pro tempore (Augustus O. Bacon) called the Senate to order and directed the Secretary to read the resolution of the Senate adopted on the 28th of January last.

The Secretary (Charles G. Bennett) read the resolution, as follows:

*Resolved,* That Saturday, the 15th day of February, be set apart for appropriate exercises in commemoration of the life, character, and public service of the late JAMES S. SHERMAN, Vice President of the United States and President of the Senate of the United States

The PRESIDENT pro tempore. The Senate is now in session for the purposes of this resolution.

At 12 o'clock and 3 minutes p. m. the Sergeant at Arms (E. L. Cornelius) announced the Speaker and Members of the House of Representatives of the United States.

The Speaker was escorted to a seat on the left of the President pro tempore, and the Members of the House of Representatives, the Clerk, Sergeant at Arms, and Chaplain of the House occupied the seats assigned them.

At 12 o'clock and 6 minutes p. m. the Sergeant at Arms announced the Chief Justice of the United States and the Associate Justices of the Supreme Court of the United

States, who were conducted to the seats provided for them in the area in front of the Secretary's desk.

At 12 o'clock and 8 minutes p. m. the Sergeant at Arms announced the ambassadors and ministers plenipotentiary from foreign countries to the United States, and they were conducted to the seats assigned them.

At 12 o'clock and 10 minutes p. m. the Sergeant at Arms announced the President of the United States and the members of his Cabinet, who were escorted to the seats provided for them in the space in front of the Secretary's desk

The other invited guests, the judges of the Commerce Court, the judges of the Court of Customs Appeals, the judges of the courts of the District of Columbia, the officers of the Army and Navy stationed in Washington, the members of the Interstate Commerce Commission, and the members of the Civil Service Commission, occupied seats on the floor of the Senate.

The PRESIDENT pro tempore Prayer will now be offered by the Chaplain of the Senate.

The Chaplain of the Senate, Rev. Ulysses G. B Pierce, D. D., offered the following prayer.

Almighty God, our heavenly Father, Thou hast been our dwelling place in all generations. Before the mountains were brought forth, or ever Thou hadst formed the earth and the world, even from everlasting to everlasting, Thou art God. We thank Thee, O Holy One, that in a world of fleeting change and where naught abides we can take refuge in Thee who inhabitest eternity. Because Thou art so great, and for that Thy years have no end, therefore canst Thou stoop even to us who seem but children of a day. Bend over us now, we beseech Thee, and for our weakness give Thou us of Thy strength, and in the darkness of our sorrow bid the light of Thy Holy Spirit to shine upon us.

[22]

Thou knowest all, our Father, and because Thou knowest Thou canst help. Thou knowest how weak and frail we are. Therefore we look unto Thee, who art Lord alike of life and of death. To Thine unfailing compassion we turn, even to Thee, who dost note Thy children's pain and sorrow. We bring to Thee our empty hearts, our loneliness, our pain, and lay them at Thy feet. If we drop a tear, it is not because we doubt Thee or because we murmur at Thy will, but because of the great love we bear to him whom Thou hast called from our visible presence and whom we this day mourn. In Thy name we consecrate this day to him.

Thou hast taken from us, our Father, the Vice President of this Nation and the President of this Senate. As we record the greatness of our loss and faintly utter our tributes of love and honor, aid Thou us. Touch Thou our lips, we pray Thee, that the measure of our hearts' affection may find utterance this day. Inspire our minds, and by Thy Holy Spirit quicken our remembrance, that the life which Thou hast taken from us may live before us as he lives before Thee

O Thou who art the Giver of every good and perfect gift, sincere and fervent thanks we render unto Thee for the life, the character, and the public service of Thy servant, the Vice President of the United States. For the fruitage of his labors, for the blessed and unfading memory of his life, for these, our Father, we thank Thee more than our lips can say. And now, that Thou hast called Thy servant to Thy nearer presence and to Thy higher service, we yield him to Thy love and keeping. May his soul rest in peace!

We commend to Thee, most merciful Father, the hearts made desolate by this loss Let the light of Thy countenance dispel the grief and gloom of the home where Thy servant was wont to dwell. Comfort, we pray Thee, the wife and family as we, alas, can not do. Touch their hearts with Thy love and heal their wounds. Though Thou leadest them through the valley of the shadow of death, may they fear no evil. Let the rod of Thy faithfulness and the staff of Thy loving-kindness comfort them Give unto them beauty for ashes, the oil of joy for mourning, and the garment of praise for the spirit of heaviness. Graciously grant that neither life with its burdens nor death with its sorrows may be able to separate them from the love of God which is in Christ Jesus our Lord.

And now may God our Father, who hast loved us with an everlasting love and called us into His eternal kingdom in Christ, comfort our hearts and stablish them in every good word and in every good work. Unto Him be glory and honor, dominion and power, now and forevermore. Amen.

The PRESIDENT pro tempore. For the purposes of this commemoration a certain order of exercises has been adopted, in pursuance of which there will be addresses made by Senators and some of the guests on this occasion. The Chair now recognizes the senior Senator from New York [Mr Root].

# MEMORIAL ADDRESSES

## ADDRESS OF SENATOR ROOT, OF NEW YORK

Mr PRESIDENT: Vice President SHERMAN was born in the city of Utica, on the banks of the Mohawk, on the 24th of October, 1855. He came of English stock. His father, Richard U. Sherman, was a native of the same county and was one of its well-known and esteemed citizens. His grandfather, Willett Sherman, was one of the early settlers upon the lands relinquished by the Oneida Indians toward the close of the eighteenth century, and he was one of the first manufacturers of central New York. The grandson was graduated from Hamilton College in the class of 1878. He was admitted to the bar in 1880 and became a successful lawyer. In 1884 he was made mayor of his native city  In 1886 he was chosen by the people of the great manufacturing region of the upper Mohawk to represent them in the Fiftieth Congress, and for more than 20 years he continued to represent them with but one break in his continuous service through reelection to the Fifty-first, Fifty-third, Fifty-fourth, Fifty-fifth, Fifty-sixth, Fifty-seventh, Fifty-eighth, Fifty-ninth, and Sixtieth Congresses. He became a potent factor in the House of Representatives. He was an active member of the Committee on Interstate and Foreign Commerce; he was chairman of the Committee on Indian Affairs; and he was long a member of the Committee on Rules, one of that little group of three constituting a majority of the committee, who, under the former rules of the House, guided the course of legislation and accomplished the nearest approach to responsible parliamentary government which this country has ever seen. Through frequent designation as Chairman to preside over the House sitting in Committee of the Whole, where so great a part of the business of the House is done, he gradually rose to general recognition as a parliamentarian of the first order and a presiding officer of the highest effectiveness  In his own city, as the years passed, evidences accumulated of the respect and confidence in which a community so rarely errs while it renders unpremeditated judgment upon the character of one known through the contact and observation of daily life  He was made treasurer of his church, the Dutch Reformed Church, of Utica, and chairman of its board of trustees  He was chosen to be president of the Utica Trust & Deposit Co.  He was made a trustee of his alma mater and a member of the executive committee of its board of trustees.  Children grew up about him and the wife of his youth, in a home where virtue, family affection, cheerfulness, honor, and obedience ruled. It was one of those homes which, indefinitely multiplied among a people, are the safe foundations of just and free self-government, and sure guaranties of the future in a republic.  From near and far throughout that region the unfortunate and struggling learned to come to him, their Representative, and his kindness and ready sympathy never failed them.  No trouble of another was ever too great or too small to command his attention.  His patience under such demands was never worn out.  His willingness to take trouble for others was never overtaxed.  In the feelings of his people grateful appreciation of the poor and humble for his kindly service was mingled with general pride in the honor of his representation and of his citizenship

The long and distinguished career as a Representative in Congress was brought to a close by Mr. SHERMAN's election to the Vice Presidency in November, 1908. He was renominated by his party for the same high office in 1912, but a fatal malady already had been established, and before the election, at his home in Utica, on the 30th of October, 1912, his earthly course came to its end.

Senators know, but few outside of the Senate fully appreciate, how great a service he rendered as presiding officer in this Chamber during the three and one-half years which followed the inauguration of March, 1909. Only experience can give a full understanding of the difficulties of legislation, the obstacles to progress in legislative business presented by the persistent advocacy of a multitude of varying opinions, and the impossibility of wise and judicious consideration when feelings are exasperated and personal prejudices and antipathies are excited. Only through experience can one learn how much the success of legislative consideration depends upon the spirit which pervades the legislative chamber, and how much depends upon the firm and intelligent application of those rules of procedure which the experience of centuries has shown to be necessary in the conduct of legislation. During all the years in which Vice President SHERMAN presided over the Senate we felt the calming and steadying effect of a serene and potent presence in the chair. The justice of his rulings was the product not merely of intellectual integrity, but also of essential kindliness of feeling and consideration. Not only the rulings were fair, but the man was fair. He was strong and self-possessed and untroubled, with a gentle and delicate sense of humor subdued to the proprieties of the place, with swift certainty of conclusion, founded upon knowledge and accurate thinking, carrying conviction and making acquiescence natural. He expedited business by always doing promptly the right thing without vacillation or delay. In the rare instances when he found himself mistaken, prompt acknowledgment and reparation were accorded with such frank sincerity that the sufferer by the mistake felt himself the gainer. He was positive without dogmatism; certain without personal overconfidence. He controlled procedure under the rules without making them the instruments of irritation or oppression, and without sacrificing the spirit to the letter. Senators of all parties became his friends. All lamented his untimely death, and all join here in doing honor to his memory.

All associated action among men exhibits an inevitable conflict between the idea of combined efficiency and the idea of individual freedom. Neither can prevail without some sacrifice of the other. The difference is temperamental, and the two types of character are hard to reconcile and are prone to misjudgment, each of the other.

Mr. SHERMAN was of the type which seeks efficiency by the law of its nature   His instincts were for order, discipline, intelligent direction, voluntary subordination to a common purpose, definite conclusions, achievement. So in politics, from first to last, he was always for party organization and party responsibility. In the House he was always for the most effective rules of procedure, and as a parliamentary presiding officer he naturally made the application of parliamentary rules a means of progress rather than an obstacle. His character exhibited in high degree the virtues of his type. He had the capacity for sympathetic appreciation of the feelings and motives of others which makes associated action easy. He had a genius for friendship which conciliated affection and disarmed enmity. He thought much of the common cause in which he was enlisted and little of his own advantage; much of general success and little of personal advancement. He was modest and unassuming—never vaunted himself or pressed himself forward. He never sought the spotlight on the public stage. He was free from the exaggerated egoism which has wrecked so many fair causes. He had the unselfishness and self-control to obey where others rightly led, and he had the clearness of intelligence, the force of personality, and the decision of character to lead, so that others might follow. He was simple and direct in thought and action. He was frank and truthful and entirely free from that cowardice which breeds deception. He had naturally an unconscious courage which needed no screwing up to the sticking point. Among all the multitude who have known him, in boyhood and in manhood, in private and in public, not one can recall a mean or ignoble or cruel or deceitful word or act on his part. He was sincere in his beliefs, he was faithful to his word, he was steadfast in his friendships, he was loyal to every cause that he espoused. His life made men happier; his example is making men better. His service will endure in the fabric of our institutions

In this Republic, unlike many nations which enjoy constitutional government, we grant no titles of nobility and no decorations for honor. As public servants complete their work and pass from the stage of action the judgment of their contemporaries finds no such definite means of expression, and so we have come here to-day to render in this ceremony the verdict of our generation upon the private virtues and the public service of JAMES SCHOOLCRAFT SHERMAN. The Senate and the House of Representatives, the Chief Justice and the Associate Justices of the Supreme Court, the ambassadors and ministers of foreign powers, the President and his Cabinet, the civil and military and naval officers of the Nation, a multitude of friends who knew him and of countrymen who knew him not, join here to set in the archives of our Government a record of honor which will remain so long as the Nation he served so well endures.

### Address of Senator Martin, of Virginia

Mr. President: To an orator or an essayist the aspirations, achievements, and character of the late Vice President Sherman would furnish a theme big enough and broad enough to invite and justify an effort of the most philosophic and ambitious proportions. My time, opportunity, and humble abilities have not tempted me to undertake to offer to the Senate to-day anything on that plane. My only desire is very briefly and in plain and simple words to pay some tribute to the memory of a personal friend, a patriotic citizen, and an able and upright public officer.

I knew Vice President Sherman chiefly in his relations to the Senate as its presiding officer and in his relations with Senators in his daily contact and association with them. He was elected Vice President of the United States on the 3d day of November, 1908. He took the oath of office and entered upon the discharge of his duties on the 4th day of March, 1909. On that day he first presided over the Senate. The last day on which he presided over the Senate was the 12th day of June, 1912, at which time a serious illness compelled him to discontinue his active work and go to his home at Utica, N. Y., where on the 30th day of October, 1912, he departed this life.

Between the 4th day of March, 1909, and the 12th day of June, 1912, a period of three years and more than three months, he was rarely absent from his post of duty in the Senate. During that period I can say with perfect safety that no one heard from him, either from the chair as the presiding officer of the Senate or in his association with Senators, a harsh, unkind, unjust, or unpleasant word.

The Senate during my 18 years of service in the body has been fortunate in its presiding officers, but in no instance, either of a Vice President or a President pro tempore, has the body been honored with an abler, more courteous, or more impartial presiding officer than Vice President SHERMAN. He was as just and as fair to one side of the Chamber as to the other He was as courteous, considerate, and as just to the Democrats as he was to the most conspicuous and able Republicans in the body He was by training and conviction a Republican in politics; he was always loyal to his party. He was by nature a partisan. I have no doubt I am as intense a partisan as he was, and I trust I am as devoted to the Democratic Party as he was to the Republican Party, but, Mr. President, in the Senate there is much less of politics than is generally supposed to exist.

In respect to questions essentially political in their nature Senators divide on political lines, but questions of that character constitute only a very small per cent of the questions which come before the Senate; and in defining questions essentially and properly political I would limit them to questions in respect to which Senators form their opinions in accordance with their convictions as to the policies in their judgment most promotive of the public welfare. In the Senate rarely, if ever, are questions treated as political questions with a view to gaining political advantages for the one party or the other. From my experience and observation in the Senate I can say I have found very little disposition on either side of the Chamber to deal with public questions with a view to party advantage rather than with a view to the public welfare. From this broad and patriotic point of view the late Vice President SHERMAN was a partisan in respect to questions essentially and properly of a political nature. So long as men adhere to this patriotic and honorable line of division on political questions politics does not and can not interfere with cordial personal relations or lead to unjust, unfair, or partial rulings from the chair. A partisan only in this higher and nobler sense, and actuated only by patriotic motives, it was inevitable that the official rulings of Vice President SHERMAN from the chair would always bear the impress of honest conviction and intelligent consideration and command the respect of Senators on both sides of the Chamber.

As his rulings were impartial as between the two political parties in the Senate, so his personal friendships were not confined to the members of either one of the political parties. He was my personal friend. My associations with him constitute one of the most pleasing features of my public life. He enjoyed to the fullest extent the confidence and esteem of the Democrats as well as of the Republicans of the Senate, and with many of them he was on terms of the closest friendship. Democrats consulted and advised with him as freely as the Republicans did. There was no sham or hypocrisy in his character. In his personal association with Senators he was always frank, cordial, and courteous. In the conduct of the business of the Senate he was attentive, vigilant, just, and able. He was a careful student of parliamentary law, and in his rulings rarely, if ever, erred; but whether he erred or not, there was never an occasion during his official life in the Senate when any Senator questioned his fidelity of purpose or his careful consideration of any question presented to him or his earnest desire to dispose of it correctly and justly

His death brought the deepest sorrow to every Member of this body. In the official business of the Senate he has been missed more than words can reasonably express. The country at large has lost one of its noblest citizens and a public officer of the highest ideals, devoted to the faithful discharge of every duty devolved upon him.

Mr PRESIDENT: When on a certain occasion the late Vice President called me to the desk, saying that he felt ill, and asked me to take the chair for the remainder of the day, he added, with pathos in his voice, " I am not at all sure how long I shall be able to continue to preside over the Senate." He then told me something of his fears, and as he left the Chamber my heart sank, and what followed a little later was not a matter of complete surprise to me. As was his custom in emergencies, Mr. SHERMAN made a brave fight against the disease that had fastened itself upon him, and only surrendered when poor, weak human nature succumbed to the inevitable.

JAMES SCHOOLCRAFT SHERMAN was a strong type of the best in our public life. He was an intelligent legislator, an ideal presiding officer, a powerful debater, and an orator of acknowledged ability. He was a good friend, a charming companion, and a loving husband and father, whose popularity was nation-wide. His death was a shock not only to his countrymen, but beyond our borders it was felt as a calamity. He died as serenely and bravely as he lived.

Mr President, the predominant note in Mr SHERMAN's life was geniality and good nature. From him radiated a sweetness and tenderness that were contagious. No one came in contact with him without feeling the influence of a pure, generous, lovable soul. He was kind to animals, fond of sports, and a lover of nature. In good literature he found great pleasure, and in the study of economic questions he took special delight.

In both Houses of Congress Mr. SHERMAN was universally liked, and in every relation of life he was honored and respected. We sadly miss him from this Chamber, where he was held in highest esteem by the entire membership. While a strong party man, he was free from narrow partisanship He was in the truest sense a patriot, loving his country and its institutions, and devoted to the happiness and welfare of all classes of its people. He was broad-minded and large-hearted, incapable of a meanness, and filled with sympathy and love for his fellows. Such a life surely did not end when death came. Rather let us believe that it was the beginning of a higher and better existence, and that the earthly activities of our friend were but the prelude to a life of greater beauty, of grander aspirations, and of nobler achievements. In the contemplation of the great mystery that surrounds death and immortality, which no one, however wise, can fully interpret, we may well exclaim·

> Shall I say that what heaven gave
> Earth has taken?
> Or that sleepers in the grave
> Reawaken?
> One sole sentence can I know,
> Can I say:
> You, my comrade, had to go,
> I to stay.

And so, Mr. President, to this brief and inadequate tribute to a dear friend, whose memory will always be lovingly treasured in my heart of hearts, I can but add the simple word " adieu."

### Address of Senator Thornton, of Louisiana

Mr. President. It is to me a source of mingled sorrow and pleasure to have been asked to speak on this occasion.

Of sorrow, because it brings freshly to my mind the thought of the loss of him whose memory we are assembled to honor, and of pleasure because of the opportunity given me to add my short tribute of respect and affection to the fuller tributes placed on the altar of his memory this day.

It was not my good fortune to know him as long as did others who have preceded or will follow me, but I shall ever esteem it fortunate for me that I knew him at all.

My acquaintance with Mr Sherman only dated from my entrance into the Senate in 1910, yet in the time that I knew him I learned to love him because of his sweet spirit, his gracious demeanor, his kindly consideration, coupled with the fine sense of humor that added to the charm of his personality and made his companionship so agreeable.

These were the traits of character that won my heart soon after we met and held it to the end.

And it is not on the statesman, the Congressman, the presiding officer of the Senate, or the Vice President of the United States that my mind lovingly dwells, but on the lovable man.

And I do not know how better to illustrate these winning qualities I have mentioned and the recognition by others of their exercise than by relating an incident in which he and I were the actors and the comment of a third party thereon.

[35]

He was not presiding over the Senate on the morning I was sworn in, and I did not meet him for four days thereafter  Then he came to my seat and, with that pleasant smile we all so well remember, said: "Senator, I have not had the opportunity of making your acquaintance, but I wish now to introduce myself and so say that I welcome you to the Senate and hope your stay with us will be always agreeable and pleasant to you."

And after a moment of pleasant chat he left, taking a part of my heart with him

About a day after this little incident, one of my Democratic friends from the House of Representatives, who had seen long service in that body with Mr. Sherman and was on intimate personal terms with him, came over to the Senate and sat down by me and said  "Have you met my friend, Jim Sherman, yet?"  Then I told him of the incident of the previous day and of how much I had appreciated the gracious action, and his comment was: "Now is not that exactly like Jim Sherman!"

This was the beginning of my acquaintance with him, this the first of the many acts of kindness shown me by him during the two years that followed until death stayed the hand always so ready to be uplifted for the help of others

And so it was that I learned to love him while he was here, and so it is that I shall love his memory since he has gone.

And I am sure that my experience with him is that of all with whom he came in contact, for he was filled with the spirit of kindness toward others, and many there are besides myself who loved him living and mourn him dead  And if the beautiful dream of the poet be true, that on the roll of the book of gold hereafter the names of those who loved their fellow men shall be first inscribed, then will his name be found high up on the list.

We will no more see the winning smile, no more feel the cordial hand grasp, no more receive the acts of kindly sympathy, but the memory of it all will remain with us and make us feel thankful that we knew one whose impulses through life prompted his conduct toward others to the end that he might contribute to their happiness

### Address of Senator Lodge, of Massachusetts

Mr. President: The tie which binds those who have been long together in the public service is apt to grow very close as the years glide by.  Mr. Sherman and I,, as it chanced, began our congressional life at the same time, in the Fiftieth Congress, 26 years ago  Except for two years, when he was out of the House for one term, we have been together ever since.  He remained in the House, was one of its most trusted leaders and most efficient Members.  During all those years I saw him constantly, and it was with peculiar pleasure that, as the president of the convention, I declared his nomination as the Republican candidate for the Vice Presidency in 1908.  His service here in the high office to which he was chosen is so recent that it is as fresh in our minds as the grief we have all felt for his untimely death.  I say "untimely," for he was still far from the chilling precincts of old age, and any death is premature which strikes a man down when he is in the prime of his abilities, when he is ripened by long training and wide experience, and when his life is still valuable to his country, still ample in promise for a yet larger service in the future.

Of his long and successful career as a legislator I shall not attempt to speak  Others who saw him at work year after year in the House can alone do him sufficient justice in this respect.  But there is one phase of his public work of which I wish to say a few words, because he there attained to an excellence not often reached in what is always an exacting and sometimes an ungrateful duty.  During his long service in the House he gradually came to be recognized as the best Chairman of the Committee of the Whole whom that great body had known in many years.

To preside not merely well but effectively in the House Committee of the Whole is a severe test of a man's qualities, both moral and mental  He must have strength of character as well as ability, quickness in decision must go hand in hand with knowledge, and firmness must always be accompanied by good temper.

Many if not most persons seem to regard parliamentary law as a collection of haphazard and arbitrary rules.  No view could be more erroneous  General parliamentary law, like all other systems of law or jurisprudence, rests upon certain underlying principles, and is designed to carry out those principles and to effect particular purposes for which the system exists  Parliamentary law aims to insure the transaction of business by legislative bodies, to eliminate disorder and confusion from the process, to make impossible the occurrence of situations where there is no thoroughfare and no way out, and to preserve the proper rights of minorities.

For the attainment of these objects, so essential to the transaction of business in any legislative assembly or any large body which debates and votes, parliamentary law has been developed by practice and perfected by long experience.  A presiding officer of high and marked ability like Mr. SHERMAN must therefore possess a full knowledge of the principles upon which parliamentary law is based and also understand the philosophy of the system so that he can apply it at will to any given question. Besides this familiarity with general parliamentary law and in addition to a firm grasp of its principles, a presiding officer must know thoroughly the rules of the particular body which he serves.  In the case of our House of Representatives the rules are many and complicated and the literature to which they have given rise in discussions, decisions, and precedents is voluminous in the extreme. In the Senate, on the other hand, the rules are simple and their burden is light, but they are administered in conformity with habits and customs which have slowly grown up during a century and which, for that very reason, can be understood and appreciated only by the exercise of patient and observant care. Mr. SHERMAN, as Chairman of the Committee of the Whole in the House and as President of the Senate, met the exacting and very difficult requirements of both positions with a success as complete as it is rare. He was equally master of general parliamentary practice and its principles and of the various systems peculiar to the two branches of Congress. Always alert, prompt, and clear in decision, rapid in the conduct of business, he was courtesy and kindness itself to all the Members of the House and Senate. A strong party man, of deep convictions as to political principles, when in the chair he recognized no party divisions on the floor. To him in that high and responsible place each Member of this body was simply a Senator with rights and obligations equal to those of every other Member of the body. He understood thoroughly also that most essential fact, that the first duty of a presiding officer is to preside, and, when questions of order are raised, to decide. He realized fully that it was far better to run the risk of an occasional error, against which his knowledge and experience protected him, than, like Lord Eldon, to say continually "I doubt." He knew that the presiding officer who hesitates is, if not always lost, quite sure to find control of the helm slipping from him, to see the public business drift off on the baffling waves of debate, ground on the shoals of delay, or sink, a helpless wreck, even when in sight of land   Therefore he ruled, as he conducted the general business, clearly and without doubt or hesitation.

He exhibited also in a high degree, whenever occasion demanded, the steady courage which is at all times so important, but which is not always associated in the minds of most people with the qualifications of a presiding officer   Correct rulings may readily be as unpopular as a righteous vote or an honest speech, and it is very easy to create a doubt under cover of which the unpopular ruling can be escaped.   This Mr. SHERMAN never did.   He was as incapable of making a wrong ruling through fear as he was of ruling wrongly to advance a personal or party interest.   I remember well one occasion when a very popular and much-desired amendment was offered to an appropriation bill where it was plainly out of order   Under the Senate rules the Chair may submit a question of order to the Senate.   It was not necessary in this instance that Mr. SHERMAN should rule wrongly, it was only necessary to stand back and allow the Senate to set the rule aside.   Mr. SHERMAN was urged to submit the question of order to the Senate.   He declined to do so.   He refused to evade his duty.   The point of order was made, and he sustained it.   It was not popular to do this, but it was right, and the act showed not only courage but a high conception of public duty.

I have dwelt upon this single phase of Mr SHERMAN's public service, because time forbids that I should do more, and because the high excellence which he achieved as a presiding officer, both in the House and Senate, is in itself at once an exhibition and a proof of his ability, his intellectual keenness, and his force of character.   But I can not end these most inadequate words without speaking of him for an instant as a friend and wholly apart from his public service.   He was one of the best and most loyal friends   Indeed, his loyalty to a friend was so strong that he more than once bore troubles not his own and endured censure when he had no fault, rather than desert one to whom his friendship had been given. He was one of the pleasantest and most agreeable of companions, full of fun and humor, and with a sympathetic interest which ranged over many subjects and touched many men. By those who knew him well he is greatly missed. Not a day goes by that I do not think of him here and of our talks together, that I do not wish I could hear once again that hearty laugh and cheery voice, that I could see him as he was, now serious, now mirthful, but always strong and kind and full of sympathy with those for whom he cared. He died in the highest office but one of the Republic. The office will be filled, but the place which he had made for himself in the affection of those who knew him will remain vacant and unoccupied.

## ADDRESS OF SENATOR KERN, OF INDIANA

Mr. PRESIDENT It was during the presidential campaign of 1908, and in the city of Chicago, that I first met JAMES S SHERMAN. We were opposing candidates for Vice President, and at that particular time and place the political situation was the subject of well-nigh universal discussion. Both of us were in the midst of the contest. I have never forgotten the genial warmth of Mr. SHERMAN's greeting, and the ease with which he captured my friendship.

Before that meeting I had him in mind as a formidable political adversary—a foeman worthy the steel of any man, but none the less a foeman. After looking into his genial face, which reflected that gentle spirit, and hearing his words of kindly greeting which so clearly proceeded from a heart full of affection for his fellow men I was never able to regard him otherwise than as my friend

Some weeks later as the campaign proceeded I was about to be introduced to a very large political assemblage in his home city of Utica, when a telegram was handed me It was from Mr SHERMAN, who was in a distant part of the country, bidding me welcome to his city, expressing his hearty good will, and urging me to call upon his family while in Utica.

A few days later, when the word came to me that a member of my family had been suddenly stricken by disease, I had scarcely turned my face toward home, abandoning the campaign for a time, when from my opponent, this great-hearted man, came a message full of sympathy, expressing in tenderest phrase his hopes that my worst fears might not be realized

Within a week of the election, when a foul libel assailing my reputation had been published in a single eastern newspaper, the first knowledge I had of the article came from Mr. SHERMAN, deprecating the publication and reassuring me of his high personal regard

When I came to the Senate two years ago he was so anxious to show his good will and emphasize his personal friendship that within five minutes after the oath had been administered to me he invited me to take the gavel and preside over the Senate. I protested that I was a stranger, not only to this body but its procedure, but he insisted, saying, " It will be only for a few minutes and it is for my own pleasure and gratification that I ask you to do me this personal favor "

And from that time on until the last he never lost an opportunity to make me feel that however wide our political differences—and they were irreconcilable—I had in him a friend on whose fidelity I might always rely.

Such incidents may be tiresome, in so far as they refer to my personal connection with them, but it seemed to me that the recital of these bare facts would serve to illustrate the kindness of heart and nobility of spirit of this man whose untimely death we mourn, with far greater force than I could possibly portray them in any combination of words, however ingeniously arranged or eloquently expressed

While the election of 1908 brought to me defeat, disastrous as such things are counted or measured amongst men, the campaign brought to me in the nature of recompense the friendship of this man, which during his life I treasured as one of my dearest possessions, and now that he has " gone forever and ever by," the memory of that friendship will bless and inspire me to my latest day.

There are men here who knew him intimately throughout his long and honorable public career, covering a period of nearly a quarter of a century, and who, therefore, must have loved him well, but I doubt if any of such men had greater reason than I for yielding to him a full measure of affectionate regard or who felt a deeper sense of personal loss when death took from me such a friend.

It is not my purpose to speak of this man's official life, nor of the distinction gained by him during his years of service as a Representative in Congress of a rich and populous district, or those other years of service here as the Vice President of the United States

The people of the Utica district honored and trusted him, and he was altogether faithful to their interests. They loved him, and he gave them his personal affection in return. He won their continued support by his fidelity to duty, but he won their hearts by his unfailing kindness and gentle bearing to everyone

And so in this body. As a presiding officer he was able and impartial, and because of the ability with which he discharged the duties of his high office he was honored by the Senators from every State And yet when he died and a deep sense of personal loss and bereavement oppressed us, it was not of his great ability as a presiding officer, or the loss that the Nation had sustained in the loss of its Vice President, that we thought first, but rather of the great heart of the man, of his genial manners, his gentle ways, and his never-failing love for his fellow man.

His public record is one of which his family and friends may be justly proud He will be doubtless remembered as a commanding figure in the councils of the Nation in that period during which he served the people. But beyond and above all this, the memories of his cheery smile, his kindly deeds, his generous conduct toward political friend and foe alike, which made men love him, will find their way into the history of the times in which he lived, and in the homes of the people at least will add luster to his name.

It is better that a man should have the personal affection of the hundreds who know him well and love him for the sweetness of his life and character than that he should have the applause of the millions because of great public achievements, while hungering for the joys of personal friendship of which he knows nothing

The Divine Master when on earth, being called upon for a solution of the problem as to what was necessary in the conduct of man to insure the inheritance of eternal life, declared that he who loved God and who also loved his neighbor as himself should surely live, and in further exemplification of the law of love which glorified the new dispensation declared · "A new commandment I give unto you, that ye love one another"

What a true disciple of this Christian doctrine, what a consistent follower of these divine teachings, was the late Vice President of the United States!

And if we may rely upon the teachings and promises of the Man of Galilee, as with confidence we do, then is the future of our friend assured, for he has come into that inheritance of eternal life which has been promised to all who, keeping God's commands, have loved their fellow men.

### Address of Senator La Follette, of Wisconsin

Mr. President: In the brief time assigned me I can offer but the simplest tribute to a personal friend.

I first met the late Vice President 25 years ago, when he became a Member of the Fiftieth Congress. I had entered the House of Representatives two years before. We were of the same age. We were both Republicans. We became friends. We served together four years. We were both retired from the public service on the 4th of March, 1891. We did not meet again for 15 years.

In those intervening years he had been returned to the House of Representatives, where he had risen to position and to power. I had gone back to my State, to find another call to service.

When we again met in this Chamber, a decade and a half had wrought great changes in political parties and in the country. We were both Republicans, but he was of one school, I of another. He believed that the interests of business and the interests of the country were at all times identical. I believed otherwise. But while we disagreed on many if not most matters of legislation, our friendly personal relations remained unbroken to the end.

Looking back upon the years in which he laid the foundations of his career, I can well understand its influence upon his conception of the obligations of public service. The strongest men are, in some degree at least, the product of their environment. But whatever may have been the influences directing the course of Mr. Sherman's thinking, that course was a steadfast and consistent one throughout his life. His convictions were strong and

[47]

were strongly maintained. He never skulked or evaded, but with resolution and courage fought out every issue openly, to victory or to defeat

From the House of Representatives he was chosen to be Vice President of the United States. But in the hour of his greatest triumph, when life and hope were strongest within, the hand of death was laid upon him. At the very threshold of his new career the grim messenger met him. From the first its shadow went with him in and out of this Chamber, stood over him at his desk, followed him down the corridors, pursued him to his home. Month after month, waking or sleeping, in social cheer or the still hours of the night, it was his constant companion. Before all others he was the first to know what threatened him. His ear first caught the mandate that chills the heart and slows the pulse: "Be ye ready, the summons cometh quickly."

He indulged in no delusions touching the final issue. His clear vision saw straight to the open tomb. To go down in defeat and to rise again and fight on demands courage of a high order. To face death when it breaks life off in the middle and to make no sign is the supreme test.

He understood  But he took care that those who were nearest and dearest to him should not know  He bore an outward geniality and spirit that dispelled fear from all his friends, while caring for every detail, and making the final preparation.

Mr. President, the longest span of life is but a day— a day of sunshine and shadow between the impenetrable darkness of two eternities  The mystery of our coming and going we can not solve, but—

> We believe that God is overhead,
> And as life is to the living,
> So death is to the dead

ADDRESS OF SENATOR WILLIAMS, OF MISSISSIPPI

Mr President: Mr James S. Sherman, Vice President of the United States, was cut down in the high tide of physical and mental virility and maturity

Shakespeare pictures life as a one-act play with seven scenes, and of the seventh he says:

> Last scene of all,
> That ends this strange eventful history,
> Is second childishness and mere oblivion,
> Sans teeth, sans eyes, sans taste, sans everything.

The man whose personality we recall to-day least of all men would have desired to live that long Rather was his temperament that of one who would heed the admonition·

> Gather ye rosebuds while ye may,
> Old Time is still a-flying,
> And this same flower that smiles to-day
> To-morrow will be dying

For that reason was he called " Sunny Jim " He was sunny in appearance, in speech, in thought, in feeling. But it was not the rippling sunniness of short, breaking wavelets on the surface of a shallow brook; the stream of his thought was deep and strong and steady.

I first met him in 1893, when both of us were Members of the Fifty-third Congress We were of totally opposite schools of political thought, opposite heredities and environments, but we soon became warm personal friends of that type who are said to be " hail fellows well met," extending one to the other every possible personal courtesy, and in legislative work every possible favor consistent with our respective partisan obligations. He was experienced, I not, and so it came to pass that he showed me how to do things in a parliamentary way. In 20 years' acquaintance I never saw a frown on his face, nor did I ever see a shadow or a cloud. He must have had his sorrows and troubles, as all of us have, but whatever they were he never afflicted others with them He shared his enjoyments, not his worries, with his friends

He had been when I first met him already a Member of two Congresses—the Fiftieth and the Fifty-first—though defeated for the Fifty-second He was after the Fifty-third a Member successively of seven more Congresses, and then for nearly four years Vice President of the United States. "He wore his honors meekly" Pride of office was as alien to him as taking himself too seriously in any other way would have been. Among his fellows he did his work patiently, vigilantly, intelligently, genially, and, above all, equably—never seeking the first place for glory nor the last to shirk labor or responsibility, but meeting with marked ability whatever fell to him as his share in his country's or his party's tasks in that great arena of struggling and often excited gladiators—the House of Representatives. The favorite of three Speakers—Reed, Henderson, and Cannon—all of whom, when forced to leave the chair at critical moments demanding a quick, decisive, self-possessed, and able parliamentarian in their stead, delighted to call him to it, he yet never held a committee assignment in the House higher than that of Judiciary at one time and Interstate and Foreign Commerce at another. For years he could have had a place on Ways and Means or Appropriations—the two leading committees there—for the asking But there were always friends who wanted preferment, and he always subordinated himself to them, thereby making the task of the Speaker, who was in those days always the party leader, easier and the pathway of his friends pleasanter.

He proved himself easily equal, if not superior, wherever he was placed. He fell below the demands of no responsibility or task laid upon him. His action was decisive; his speech facile, lucid, and terse, though unpretentious. I used to think in the House that he was the ablest and the readiest presiding officer we ever had after Reed died, and that he handled bills of which he had charge on the floor more rapidly, more easily, and with clearer explanations to Members not on the committee and seeking information than any other Member.

Above all, he did all with irresistible pleasantness of demeanor and appealing modesty. When with a point of order he took a Member off his feet and the floor, he did it with a smile, which was itself an apology, as much as to say, " I hate to trouble you, old fellow, but really the business of the House must go on in an orderly and prescribed way"; or, " I hate to disturb you of all men, but this is my only way of meeting an exigency of party management" Of nearly all men I ever met, he knew best that no man has a right to take himself or his share of human work and human honors too seriously. Men are too many, the earth is too small, and other planets and solar systems are too numerous and large and earthly life is too short for that.

> Oh, why should the spirit of mortal be proud?
> Like a fast-flitting meteor, a fast-flying cloud,
> A flash of the lightning, a break of the wave,
> He passes from life to his rest in the grave.

\*     \*     \*     \*     \*     \*     \*

> And the fever called living
> Is conquered at last

After his death his friends may say that he was—

> A man that Fortune's buffets and rewards
> Has ta'en with equal thanks.

I am not an old man yet, as life is measured here in Washington, and yet there are perhaps more of the men

who were in public life when Mr. SHERMAN and I first
entered it who are now waiting to shake our hands on the
other shore than there are on this

> Friend after friend departs;
>   Who hath not lost a friend?
> There is no union here of hearts
>   That finds not here an end

\*        \*        \*        \*        \*        \*        \*

> Over the river they beckon to us—
> Loved ones who've crossed to the farther shore.

Perhaps the best thing we can do here is to so deal with
men and women, too, that we shall be neither ashamed
nor afraid to meet them hereafter  This I believe this
man did.  I have met him by the funeral bier; in the political struggle, where we crossed swords in earnest and
fateful conflict; around the banquet board.  He was
always the same and always a gentleman, in manners,
speech, and conduct  He carried sunshine with him in
this life.  Why can we not hope that he carries it with
him over there?

Of course none of us know with certainty what death is,
nor can we know except with the eye of faith.  How can
we, when we do not even know what life is or whence
it is?

> Life! I know not what thou art,
> But know that thou and I must part,
> And when or where or how we met,
> I own to me's a secret yet

Or, as another sweet singer expresses it:

> Like to the grass that's newly sprung,
> Or, like a tale that's new begun,
> Or, like the bird that's here to-day,
> Or, like the pearl'd dew of May,
> Or, like an hour, or, like a span,
> Or, like the singing of a swan—
> E'en such is man, who lives by breath,
> Is here, now there—in life and death.

[52]

But if, as I fervently believe, existence is one duration, of which what we call life is one part on this side of the dividing portal which we call death and of which what we call eternity is the part on the other side—if, as Longfellow says:

> There is no death!  What seems so is transition,
> This life of mortal breath
> Is but a suburb of the life elysian,
> Whose portal we call Death.

Or if, as another sings—

> The living are the only dead;
> The dead live, never more to die—

then, why in sweet Heaven's name can we not go through life as JAMES S. SHERMAN did, with smiles upon our faces, meeting our tasks earnestly and honestly, but cheerfully, not sadly—doing our best and leaving the sad faults and sins of us, like little children, to the pity of the All Father whose mysteriously weak and strong and unfathomable creatures we are?

The body of him has been laid away in " God's acre "—I like that ancient Saxon phrase which calls the burial ground God's acre, it is just—and though a Nation here, through us, its representatives, is met with fit observance to do him ceremonious honor—all deserved by faithful, long, honest, intelligent public service, deserved by courteous, kind-hearted human serviceableness and cleanness in private life—I do not think he wants us to be sad or to make others sad in his death, except in so far as we can not help it because of the mutual missing of him. It is for the living who have been left by the loving and beloved dead and not for the dead themselves that we are called to sorrow, because, as to him who has passed the portal where this " mortal coil," the flesh, is " shuffled off," a freer and a broader life, untrammeled by flesh limitations and undeflected by flesh temptations, begins.

> The soul, immortal as its Sire,
> Shall never die.

[53]

### Address of Senator Curtis, of Kansas

Mr President: No one outside his family circle felt more than did I the death of James S. Sherman, the Vice President of the United States. For years I was associated with him in the House of Representatives, and early learned not only to respect him but to love him. His qualities not alone as a man, as a legislator, as a parliamentarian, but as a friend, impressed themselves upon me and quickly endeared him to me in many ways, and that endearment deepened as time went by. Mr. Sherman was more than a friendly acquaintance to those with whom he frequently came in contact. He was a fatherly man. He was at once interested in the things in which you were interested, and immediately took upon himself the cloak of helper and adviser. He was thus particularly useful and congenial to new Members, and commanded for himself respect and support in everything he undertook. In fact, I believe, and make bold at this time to assert, that James S Sherman enjoyed the real loving friendship and affection of more men throughout the country than any other one American living He had traveled extensively in the United States, and there was scarcely a town in this broad Nation in which he might appear, whether or not his coming had been heralded, that some man would not step to his side, and, throwing his arm about his neck, accost him in terms of pleasure and of attachment

Long and close association with Mr Sherman in the House gave me keen appreciation of his talents as a legislator, while all of you here to-day are aware of his exceptional abilities as a presiding officer and as an exponent of parliamentary law. While seeking no recognition as an orator, he was ready in debate, and, though kindly and considerate to his opponents on the floor, drove home arguments with such conciseness and good effect that defeat in a contest on legislative matters rarely overtook him. His readiness under all circumstances to gauge a situation in its true light, his quickness to take advantage of opportunities made him, to my mind, one of the most successful and best Representatives, and he was valued and complimented as such not only by the people of his district but of the United States. His efforts were not centralized or localized. As chairman of the Committee on Indian Affairs and as a leading member of the great Committee on Interstate and Foreign Commerce his field of labor was broad and varied, and in nothing did he shirk his responsibilities, but was constantly working for the enactment of legislation of a character which would inure to the benefit of the public and of those whose interests were at stake. A large number of the most important statutes born in these committees bear witness to-day to his ability and able judgment

Mr. SHERMAN was a partisan, open and unequivocal. He made plain his position on public policies and public questions at every opportunity, and rather, I always thought, enjoyed such declarations  There was never any misunderstanding as to where he stood on any question, and he would lose with grace, upholding his ideals, rather than yield to those beneath whose veneering was a desire to either please or advantage his opponent. He disliked pretense and detested dishonesty. While easy of approach and ready to listen to those who sought him, he was quick to detect and resent imposition or insincere motives. On such occasions his indignation would assert itself by vigorous expression and prompt refusal, and the discovery would rarely be forgotten.

Some of Mr. SHERMAN'S warmest friends were numbered among those who did not always agree with him either in politics or in policy. He was democratic, unostentatious, genial His sympathy was deep and easily stirred. He saw the right in all that he did, but, finding himself mistaken in any situation or degree, his acknowledgment of the fact was quick, earnest, and sincere. In fact, in private and public life Mr. SHERMAN met, as fully as it is possible to meet, every demand upon him as a citizen, a neighbor, a friend, and a statesman.

In his family relations he was particularly blessed. His enjoyment and contentment reached its height when his family was gathered about him, and its members, more than any others, will miss him as a devoted husband, loving, gentle father, and jealous protector.

It is difficult, indeed, to realize that JAMES S. SHERMAN has gone never to return. Had he been spared there were other heights which he might have reached, but after traveling well the road of service to his people, his party, and his Nation, he was stricken down in the prime of life and left us lonely and sorrowful at his demise. We miss his cordial greeting, his heartfelt hand grasp, his tender solicitude. His memory will live always and we are better for having known him. His career will ever be a shining example before the youth of our country, and the tributes paid him heretofore and to-day, though they do not add to his worth or greatness, are confessions of love, respect, and esteem on the part of those who not only knew him but who enjoyed in his presence and at his side those delightful characteristics and that personal charm which endeared him to young and old and which remained with him to the end.

He has gone. He has trod the path we shall tread when the summons comes. Let us be as well prepared in all things as was he, for the good he did lives after him. Our struggle here may be longer, yet for whatever time it be we will go on as " weary ships to their haven under the hill "

> But O! for the touch of a vanish'd hand,
> And the sound of a voice that is still!

### Address of Senator Cummins, of Iowa

Mr. President: It seems to be the way of this turbulent, fighting world of ours that in life the people, and especially the public people, are chiefly concerned with their never-ending disagreements; but in the presence of death, with its majestic and solemn harmonies, we no longer hear the noise of the conflict and we lay aside the weapons of our warfare. We are conscious then, as at no other time, of the immensity of that limitless region in which the peace of common purpose always reigns.

In his lifetime there were some things upon which the late Vice President and myself were not in accord, but now that he has joined the immortals upon the other shore my memory refuses to perform its accustomed office, and just now I am wondering what these differences were. In the stead of a recollection of controversy there comes trooping into my mind the remembrance of his noble manhood, his lofty character, his strong, keen intellect, his unsurpassed candor, his perfect fairness, and his tender heart. Into every political contest he carried not only the flawless courage but the sensitive honor of the knights in the olden time. He hit hard, but only when he was face to face with his adversary. The body of his enemy felt his blows; but the wounds he inflicted were always found on the breast, never on the back. The American people had a name for him, and they will cherish it so long as humanity holds the affection which lightens and sweetens mortal existence.

To be loved by close associates and immediate followers is a joy that many men experience, but to be loved by the whole number of one's acquaintance is a distinction that but few men have attained, and our lamented friend was one of these rare, choice spirits of the world

For nearly four years JAMES S. SHERMAN, as Vice President of the United States, was the presiding officer of the Senate. Others have spoken, and spoken well, of his service elsewhere My purpose is to record my high appreciation of his service here. The qualities which fit a man to guide the deliberations of a body like ours, to administer the rules which govern it, and to render quick justice to all its members, are rarely united in a single man High above every other quality is the power to be fair and impartial. Most men, I think, want to be fair, but there are only a few men who, in the moments of stress and storm, have the capacity to be fair. Vice President SHERMAN had this quality in as high degree as any man I ever knew. During all the time he directed our deliberations he was eminently just. So successful was he that throughout all the days of fierce debate, days in which feeling ran strong, there never arose the least suspicion of his perfect impartiality.

He was a skilled parliamentarian He was not only master of the general subject, but, what is more wonderful, he was master of the mysterious rules which we have adopted for our own government. His decisions were quickly made and were delivered with precision and emphasis. The operations of his mind were not only accurate, but they were lightninglike in their rapidity. He was courteous, but his firmness was as striking as his courtesy. Many illustrious men have occupied the chair to which he so worthily succeeded, but I venture to say that no one of them discharged its duties more faithfully or more efficiently than did he.

All in all, I have never known a presiding officer who combined all the qualities of mind and conscience demanded by such an office more completely than they were united in him; and when the Master called him he laid down the authority of his commanding position among us with the love, the respect, the confidence, and the admiration not only of every Senator but of all his fellow men

With hearts full of sorrow we say of him the best that can be said of any man—the world is better because he lived in it.

### Address of Senator Oliver, of Pennsylvania

Mr. President. Few men have lived and died who were better loved than James Schoolcraft Sherman. I leave it to those who knew him from his earlier years to tell the story of his public life, and will content myself with saying a very few words about Sherman the man—for it was as man to man that we knew each other best. I never met him until after he was Vice President and I was a Senator, not quite four years ago; but we were thrown into close companionship during the long extra session of 1909, and from that association there grew a friendship which, on my part, was at least as strong as I ever felt for any man, and I believe that on his part it was just as strong. No man could be with him long without becoming his friend His very presence compelled friendship The sunny smile which dominated his face, and about which so much has been said and written, was not the mere mask of the hail fellow well met, but the outward manifestation of an inborn and ingrained kindly nature, filled to the full with the joy of living and the delight of mingling with his fellow men. What most endeared him to men was his intense humanity. He was human all through, and he loved human kind; and those of us who were admitted to the inner cloisters of his intimacy feel that in losing him we lost a part of our own selves, and that life for us will never again be as complete a thing as it was before he was taken away.

Hypocrisy was a thing abhorrent to him, and political hypocrisy he could tolerate least of all. Not once but often have I heard him in unsparing terms denounce men in public life who, to please the passing whim of the people, advocated or supported measures or policies in which he knew they did not believe.

He was first and last a partisan, and an intense one at that; but his partisanship was in no way tainted with bitterness of spirit. It arose from the very intensity of his convictions. He believed from his heart that his country's welfare depended on the continued supremacy of his party, and he saw no path to progress but by way of its success, and with zeal unflagging and spirit undaunted, in and out of season he labored for that success. I know, for he told me more than once, that with waning health and growing years he longed to withdraw from the conflict, and spend the days that might remain to him in the companionship of the wife and sons who were the objects of his tenderest affection, but with his rare political insight he well knew that last year's fight was to be a losing one; and he would not—constituted as he was, he could not—be recreant in its adversity to the party which had honored him in the days of its triumphant prosperity So, like the true soldier that he was, he died with his face to the foe, under the standard of the party he had served so well, and in whose principles he so implicitly believed.

> He was a man, take him for all in all,
> We shall not look upon his like again.

## Address of Senator O'Gorman, of New York

Mr President· I join in the estimate of the late Vice President, which has been so eloquently pronounced by my distinguished colleague, and I share in the general grief caused by the premature closing of a career which only a few months since was rich in achievement and full of promise for the future  It is no small achievement to serve as a political leader in city, county, and State; to represent an important constituency in the National House of Representatives for 18 years, and at the end of so long a period of exacting public service to be elevated to within one step of the highest office within the gift of a free people.  In public life such was the record of James Schoolcraft Sherman.  Its mere recital is an eloquent eulogy on the character and attainments of the citizen in whose memory we now pause to pay a last tribute of affectionate respect.  It is no mere ceremonial that the Senate, over whose counsels he presided for four years, should bestow that homage which friendship and patriotism ever offered to the true man, the faithful public servant, the enlightened statesman.  During his active and useful career Mr. Sherman witnessed the mightiest strides in material development the world has ever seen  He saw the Republic grow from the chaos of Civil War to its present commanding place among the nations of the earth.  He saw the Empire State, of which he was a native son, leap forward with giant bounds, valiantly maintaining her place at the head of the mighty procession of the States of our majestic Union  His pride in the forward strides of the State and Nation was justified, for in the upbuilding of both he played the part of an active, earnest, and public-spirited citizen.

[63]

Neither a laggard nor a drone, for more than 25 years he was in the thick of the conflict which accompanies and stimulates progress  Throughout his life Mr. SHERMAN was a popular type of the American optimist, and imparted confidence and enthusiasm to all within the influence of his delightful personality.  Industrious and successful in private enterprise, he was alert and influential in public affairs, and ably contributed to that ceaseless mental combat and attrition of thought whose constant flashes light the guiding torch of civilization which illumines the pathway of liberty and law.  His impulses were generous, his sympathies broad, his intellect keen.  He was a patriot.  He loved his country and its institutions. For many years, at great personal and domestic sacrifice, he gave loyal, generous, and disinterested service to advance the public weal and uphold his country's honor He had unbounded faith in the Republic; he had unwavering confidence in his countrymen and in their attachment to the principles of liberty and their capacity to right wrongs and uproot evils.  In their active, watchful, and vigilant patriotism he saw the best security against the evils that beset all Governments.  His best tribute was the repeated expression of confidence and approbation that came to him from his fellow citizens in central New York, who knew him so well and valued his character and attainments so highly.

After years of industry and earnest effort in party council and public arena the citizen whose deeds we now commemorate was raised to the exalted station of Vice President of the United States, from which he passed with honor to the grave.

As President of the Senate he measured up to the best traditions of that high office.  No Member of this body can forget the charm of his bearing or the ability, scrupulous impartiality, and fine courtesy with which he presided over the deliberations of this Chamber. The promptness and fairness of his rulings were no small contribution to the expedition of public business, and the lucidity with which he revealed his exceptional knowledge of parliamentary law was a constant source of pleasure and gratification.

Laying no claim to the gifts of genius, he won a high place in the Nation's councils by that persistency of effort and strength of character which constitute the genius of success. Above all, he was the true American and ideal citizen in his domestic life, and by his devotion to home and family commanded the deep respect of a moral and chivalrous people. As a stream can rise no higher than its source, so a Nation can be no better than its homes. In the family circle are found those spiritual agencies which save society from corrosion and decay. Unless a nation grows morally as well as materially, spiritually as well as intellectually, its future is dark and its days are numbered. For Mr. SHERMAN's success in life we commended him, for the enviable places that he won among his fellow men we praised him, for the public honors that he earned we admired him; yet in this solemn hour, sanctified by the liberated spirit of the comrade whom we mourn, I would pay tribute to those traits of character which made the loving husband, the devoted father, the faithful friend, the good citizen These were the titles that he won; they were the flowers of love and duty and friendship that blossomed along his pathway through life. They constitute the fairest garland that can be placed upon his tomb.

Mr. President, our departed friend gave his best to the service of the people. Who can do more? The State of New York has given many of her sons to the service of the Nation, and high upon her roll of fame posterity will inscribe the high character and unblemished record of JAMES SCHOOLCRAFT SHERMAN.

## ADDRESS OF SPEAKER CLARK, OF THE HOUSE OF REPRESENTATIVES

The PRESIDENT pro tempore. The Chair now recognizes the Speaker of the House of Representatives.

Mr PRESIDENT· Of all the wise and salutary things done by the fathers of the Republic, one of the wisest and most salutary was dividing Congress into two bodies

There is a House habit and a Senate habit, differing widely. This difference grows out of the difference in numbers, the difference in average age, and the difference in the length of tenure. Some Representatives never learn the House habit; some Senators never learn the Senate habit; a few observant men learn both habits. That Mr. Vice President SHERMAN learned both habits thoroughly and well is sufficiently attested by the fact that he presided with eminent success over the large and tumultuous assembly of the House of Representatives and over the smaller and more sedate assembly of the Senate.

I hope that it will not be taken as an ungracious word for me to suggest to Senators that JAMES SCHOOLCRAFT SHERMAN was a House product. We trained him; we gave him his promotion; we sent him to the service of the Nation in his capacity of Vice President.

There is no finer school under the sun than the House of Representatives for mental pugilistics. Personally we are courteous to each other, but there is no such thing as House courtesy that influences the course of legislation.

It might be well to state for a moment how reputations are made in the House  They are made in two ways— one by a brilliant oratorical performance and the other by assiduous industry in the committees and on the floor of the House.  I used to divide the membership with ref-

[66]

erence to rising in the House into two classes—the quick climbers and the steady climbers.

A few men make a national reputation in that House by one great oration. I saw Lafe Pence, of Colorado, in the Fifty-third Congress, make a national reputation the second day after he was sworn in, and I saw Charles E. Littlefield, of Maine, make a national reputation by one great oration within about three months of the time when he was sworn in; but these are exceptional cases As a rule, the men who achieve high position in the House do so by slow and steady climbing. Vice President SHERMAN went up and up in the House gradually until he got into the front rank. One day, in a hot political debate there, I dubbed the small coterie to which he belonged as the "Big Five," a name which stuck.

There is much truth in Longfellow's lines·

> The heights by great men reached and kept
> Were not attained by sudden flight,
> But they while their companions slept
> Were toiling upward in the night

That was the case with Mr. SHERMAN. He presided in the House and also in the Senate with grace, firmness, fairness, unfailing courtesy, rare good sense, and to the entire satisfaction of Representatives and of Senators. Though he was never elected Speaker, he was frequently assigned by three Speakers to preside temporarily over the House proper as well as over the Committee of the Whole.

While not an orator, he was a strong debater and illumined every subject which he discussed; because he never spoke on any subject on which he was not well informed—an example which all public speakers would do excellently well to follow.

A fine stage presence, graceful gestures, most gracious manners, a musical, well-modulated voice of good carrying power, exquisite taste in the selection and arrangement of words, enabled him to please the House of Representatives, the most critical and at the same time the fairest and justest audience in the wide, wide world. Though he killed the pet bills of many Members, he had not an enemy in the membership of the House. He seemed to have taken for the basis of his action the saying of Thackeray that " the world is like a looking-glass. Smile at it, and it smiles back; scowl at it, and it scowls back, hit at it, and it hits back."

He was a most successful pilot of measures through the House, the chief reason being that he moved on lines of least resistance. Adhering to his opinions with tenacity, fidelity, and courage, he antagonized no one unnecessarily. To use a common and expressive sentence, he took things by the smooth handle, and thereby accomplished much

Amiability was the chief characteristic of the man, and, after all, Tennyson was right when he said:

> Kind hearts are more than coronets,
> And simple faith than Norman blood.

Whether in committee or on the floor or in the chair, like charity, as described by St. Paul in his splendid rhapsody in the thirteenth chapter of First Corinthians, he suffered long and was kind, envied not; vaunted not himself; was not puffed up; behaved himself not unseemly, was not easily provoked In fact, he had himself so well in hand that he could not be baited into an exhibition of bad temper. He gave sharp blows, and received them with perfect equanimity. In victory he was not offensively jubilant; in defeat he was not utterly cast down. He appeared equal to both extremes of fortune, clearly realizing, with his optimistic philosophy, the astounding swiftness with which political situations change in this rapid age.

In the House he was a prime favorite on both sides of the big aisle, which constitutes the line of demarcation in politics, but not in personal friendships or robust Americanism. When he was translated from that energetic and boisterous body to the dignity and quietude of the Vice Presidency his fellow members, while sincerely rejoicing at his promotion, just as sincerely regretted his departure from their midst.

The House most heartily joins the Senate and the President of the United States in doing honor to this typical American. His fitting epitaph would be.

*Mens aequa in arduis.*

## ADDRESS OF PRESIDENT TAFT

The PRESIDENT pro tempore. As a fitting close to these ceremonies, the Chair now recognizes the President of the United States

Mr PRESIDENT: After the eloquent tributes that have been paid to the memory of the late Vice President SHERMAN by his associates, who knew him well, it is not for me to add anything new to that which has been said, and well said

Mr SHERMAN was a man with whom no one could come in contact without feeling better for the meeting and with a more kindly disposition toward his fellow men and the world at large

Life, on the whole, is made up of a series of what appear to many to be insignificant incidents, and there are those who in their own thoughts, in their own affairs, and in what they regard as the large issues of society recognize no necessity for attention to the daily encounters and the hourly exchanges of thought and of treatment between individuals. To them life is apparently a series of grand stage plays, which are to mark the character of the players permanently, and that which intervenes between these plays is of no importance. This view is accentuated as men grow in self-absorption and lose the sense of proportion with respect to their own importance—a weakness to which most men in greater or less degree are prone. A character that is the antithesis of such tendencies makes for himself a place among all with whom he has personal association that is durable and fragrant This was one of the lovable and most marked traits of Mr. SHERMAN. Everyone, high or low, intimate or distant, who met him, felt the influence of his good will, of his earnest desire to accord to each one the courtesy and recognition of his right as a member of society to which he was entitled. Any painful feeling that he had to cause by what duty required him to say was as painful to him as it was to the person to whom he felt called upon in this way to speak.

He never exaggerated his own importance. He deprecated the personal equation. He was always for helping a cause or some other person, and he had truly that charity and love of his fellow men which, as the poem has it, is really the love of God, and made the name of Abou Ben Adhem lead all the rest.

Educated at one of those truly American small colleges, with high patriotic ideals, derived from the history of the struggle for liberty regulated by law as embodied in our Constitution, Mr. SHERMAN came to manhood to the study and successful practice of law, but in a few years drifted, as so many country lawyers do, into politics. He loved politics; he correctly thought that he could be engaged in nothing more useful to his country, and he became a partisan on principle. As might be expected from one of his generous self-deprecatory attitude of mind, he minimized the personal and exalted his party cause. He came to believe thoroughly and, in my judgment, rightly that the only possible means of securing effective, permanent, and just popular government, truly representative of the people, is through parties, and therefore he was willing to give up much of his personal judgment to reconcile the views of himself and his associates upon a few great principles.

His personal popularity carried him into the mayoralty of the city of his birth, in which he lived his life long. Then he came to Congress, and for 20 years he was a Member, and a prominent member of the Republican

Party, in the great popular House of Representatives. There he exhibited great ability as a debater and legislator, which his fellows fully recognized. But in contemporary history Mr. SHERMAN suffers in comparison with others less deserving, because the work that he wrought, the influence that he exerted, the progress and reforms that he helped to bring about, were not recorded in the headlines of newspapers, or, indeed, in the news columns or editorials, for he was content to work quietly to achieve an object, and made no conditions that should attach his name to the success of the work in hand.

He was an influential and leading Member of that body during the controversies that took place over the question whether the House of Representatives should be permitted to do business or should be at the mercy of the minority, and he stood with one of the great Speakers of that body for progress, and it was achieved.

He was at the head of the Indian Committee in the House, and no problems in our Government are more difficult than those within the jurisdiction of that committee. They involve the proper, businesslike consideration and disposition of questions of the management of trust property in which the discretion of the particular official having control can be very little restricted by law. Conditions in and near the Indian country are such that neighboring public opinion can not be trusted to do justice to the Indians or to carry out the charitable purposes of the Government. The situation is prolific of schemes to defraud the wards of the Nation.

No one will know, except those most intimate with the course of legislation and with the details of appropriation bills, the work JAMES S. SHERMAN and a few of his associates did in the elimination of fraud and the maintenance of the honor of the Nation in preserving to the Indians what was theirs. And thus we may say truly that the great work that the man whose early death we deplore did for his fellow men was done as an adviser, as a quiet but active worker in the shadow of some more conspicuous person, all arising from the disinterested patriotism, the high-minded party spirit, and the inherent modesty of the man.

I need not recite to those who had so much better opportunity than I to observe it and feel it the clear and rapid thought and the equally clear and rapid expression of decision which in the administration of the parliamentary law that Mr. SHERMAN displayed frequently as the presiding officer of the House of Representatives and continuously during his term as Vice President as President of the Senate. He was a model presiding officer. Preserving his temper under all conditions, and some of them most difficult, he ruled with firmness and with a courtesy that disarmed the sometime heat of those whose views he was overruling

And now there is but one more word to speak, and that one utters in the tenderest tone and makes most brief. What might be expected from a man of his heart and his constant appreciation of the feelings of others, from one of nature's gentlemen, his domestic life, his love of wife and children and fellow townsmen, made a circle so sweet, a home so bright, a neighborhood so full of love for him that even in the few hours that we were permitted to spend in the city where he lived and died the overwhelming evidences of affection for him were most impressive on every hand, and his great qualities were revealed in a most remarkable tribute which his memory called out from his beloved pastor, the president of Hamilton College.

We have celebrated the memorial of a modest American, a distinguished patriot, an able statesman, a noble man!

Mr ROOT. I now move that, after the guests of the Senate shall have retired, the Senate, as a further mark of respect to the memory of the late Vice President, stand in recess until 12 o'clock noon, on Monday, the 17th of February.

The PRESIDENT pro tempore. Before submitting the motion, the Chair will give opportunity, as indicated by the Senator from New York, for the guests of the Senate to retire. The Sergeant at Arms will announce the order in which they will retire, so that they may do so without confusion.

The President of the United States and the members of his Cabinet, the ambassadors and ministers plenipotentiary to the United States, the Chief Justice and Associate Justices of the Supreme Court of the United States, the Speaker and Members of the House of Representatives, and the other guests of the Senate thereupon retired from the Chamber.

The PRESIDENT pro tempore. The Senator from New York [Mr Root] moves that, as a further mark of respect, the Senate now stand in recess until 12 o'clock on Monday.

The motion was unanimously agreed to; and (at 2 o'clock and 30 minutes p. m , Saturday, February 15) the Senate took a recess until Monday, February 17, 1913, at 12 o'clock meridian.

MONDAY, *February 17, 1913.*

Mr. SMOOT submitted the following concurrent resolution (S. Con. Res. 41), which was read, considered by unanimous consent, and agreed to:

*Resolved by the Senate (the House of Representatives concurring),* That there shall be printed and bound, under the direction of the Joint Committee on Printing, 14,100 copies of the proceedings and the eulogies delivered in Congress on JAMES SCHOOLCRAFT SHERMAN, late Vice President of the United States, with illustration, of which 4,000 copies shall be for the use of the Senate,

8,000 copies for the use of the House of Representatives, 2,000 copies for the use of the Senators and Representatives of the State of New York, and 100 copies, bound in full morocco, for the use of Mrs. James Schoolcraft Sherman *Provided*, That there shall be included in such publication the proclamation of the President and the proceedings in the Supreme Court of the United States upon the death of Vice President SHERMAN, and an account of the funeral services at Utica, N. Y.

## PROCEEDINGS IN THE HOUSE

The Speaker on October 31, 1912, appointed the following committee to represent the House at the funeral of the late Vice President, the Hon JAMES SCHOOLCRAFT SHERMAN:

Representatives Underwood, Alabama; Macon, Arkansas, Needham, California; Taylor, Colorado; Hill, Connecticut; Heald, Delaware; Sparkman, Florida; Bartlett, Georgia, French, Idaho; Cannon, Illinois; Crumpacker, Indiana; Murdock, Kansas; James, Kentucky; Broussard, Louisiana; Guernsey, Maine; Talbott, Maryland; McCall, Massachusetts; Hamilton, Michigan; Stevens, Minnesota; Candler, Mississippi; Bartholdt, Missouri; Pray, Montana; Kinkaid, Nebraska; Roberts, Nevada; Sulloway, New Hampshire; Gardner, New Jersey; Fergusson, New Mexico; Kitchin, North Carolina; Hanna, North Dakota; Longworth, Ohio, McGuire, Oklahoma, Hawley, Oregon; Dalzell, Pennsylvania, O'Shaunessy, Rhode Island; Finley, South Carolina; Burke, South Dakota, Moon, Tennessee;' Henry, Texas; Howell, Utah, Plumley, Vermont, Jones, Virginia; Humphrey, Washington; Hughes, West Virginia; Cooper, Wisconsin; Mondell, Wyoming; Haugen, Iowa; Payne, New York; and Hayden, Arizona.

MONDAY, *December 2, 1912*

A message from the Senate, by Mr. Crockett, one of its clerks, announced that the Senate had agreed to the following resolutions:

*Resolved,* That the Senate has heard with profound sorrow and regret the announcement of the death of JAMES SCHOOLCRAFT SHERMAN, late Vice President of the United States.

*Resolved,* That the Secretary communicate these resolutions to the House of Representatives and transmit a copy thereof to the family of the deceased.

Also:

*Resolved,* That as a further mark of respect to the memory of the late Vice President JAMES SCHOOLCRAFT SHERMAN and the late Senators Weldon Brinton Heyburn and Isidor Rayner, whose deaths have just been announced, the Senate do now adjourn.

*       *       *       *       *       *       *

Mr CANNON Mr. Speaker, I announce to the House that JAMES SCHOOLCRAFT SHERMAN, Vice President of the United States, departed this life at his home in Utica, N. Y., on the 30th day of October, 1912.

The admirable administration of the high office which he held, the second in the gift of the Republic, his brilliant and useful career for so many years in the House of Representatives, his sympathetic touch with every class, the unsullied purity of his public and private life, had so impressed the country that his death occasioned expression of deep-felt grief so universal as to manifest a general and profound sense of national bereavement.

Congress will doubtless, by concurrent action of the two Houses, at an early moment set apart a time for proper expression touching the life, character, and services of this eminent citizen.

I move you, sir, that out of regard for his memory and the memory of the Members of this House and of the Senate who have departed this life since the adjournment of the last session of Congress this House do now adjourn.

The motion was agreed to; and accordingly (at 1 o'clock and 8 minutes p m.) the House adjourned until to-morrow, Tuesday, December 3, 1912, at 12 o'clock noon.

THURSDAY, *February 6, 1913.*

Mr. FITZGERALD. Mr. Speaker, I ask unanimous consent that the Speaker lay before the House the invitation of

the Senate to attend the memorial exercises of the late
Vice President

The SPEAKER laid before the House the following resolution, which the Clerk read:

### Senate resolution 451

*Resolved*, That the Senate extend to the Speaker and the Members of the House of Representatives an invitation to attend the
exercises in commemoration of the life, character, and public
services of the late JAMES S. SHERMAN, Vice President of the
United States and President of the Senate, to be held in the Senate
Chamber on Saturday, the 15th day of February next, at 12 o'clock
noon.

Mr FITZGERALD. Mr. Speaker, I move that the invitation
be accepted, and that the Clerk be directed to notify the
Senate to that effect

The SPEAKER. The gentleman from New York moves
that the invitation of the Senate be accepted, and that the
Clerk be directed to notify the Senate to that effect.

The question was taken, and the motion was agreed to.

The following resolution, submitted by Mr. Fitzgerald,
was agreed to:

### House resolution 817

*Resolved*, That the House accept the invitation of the Senate extended to the Speaker and Members of the House of Representatives to attend the exercises in commemoration of the life, character, and public services of the late JAMES S. SHERMAN, Vice
President of the United States and President of the Senate, to be
held in the Senate Chamber on Saturday, the 15th day of February next, at 12 o'clock noon

Mr. FITZGERALD. Mr. Speaker, I ask unanimous consent
that when the House adjourns on February 14, 1913, it
adjourn to meet at 11 30 a. m. on Saturday, February 15,
1913.

The SPEAKER. The gentleman from New York asks
unanimous consent that when the House adjourns on the

14th of February, 1913, it adjourn to meet at 11.30 a. m. on Saturday, February 15, 1913. Is there objection?

There was no objection.

FRIDAY, *February 14, 1913*

Mr. FITZGERALD. Mr. Speaker, I ask unanimous consent for the present consideration of the resolution which I send to the Clerk's desk.

The Clerk read as follows.

### House resolution 835

*Resolved*, That on Saturday, February 15, 1913, at 10 minutes of 12 o'clock a. m., pursuant to the resolution heretofore adopted accepting the invitation of the Senate to attend the memorial services to commemorate the life and character and public services of the Hon. JAMES S. SHERMAN, late the Vice President of the United States, the House shall proceed, with the Speaker, to the Senate Chamber, and at the conclusion of the services it shall return to this Chamber.

The SPEAKER Is there objection to the present consideration of the resolution?

There was no objection

The resolution was agreed to.

SATURDAY, *February 15, 1913*

The House met at 11.30 a. m.

The Chaplain, Rev. Henry N. Couden, D. D., offered the following prayer:

Our Father in heaven, we thank Thee that our Republic is not ungrateful, but holds in sacred memory the men who laid her foundations deep and strong and wide; the brave men who have fought her battles, the statesmen who have breathed their spirits into her sacred institutions and kept them inviolate, as evinced by the special order of the day in memory of a noble son, who proved himself worthy of the confidence reposed in him by his fellow countrymen May his life be an incentive to faithful service and nobility of soul to those who survive him.

Be Thou solace to those who knew and loved him, and let the everlasting arms be about the bereaved wife and children, that they may look forward with confidence to the unchanging love of a heavenly Father who doeth all things well. Amen.

The Journal of the proceedings of yesterday was read and approved.

The SPEAKER The hour of 10 minutes of 12 having arrived, the House will proceed to the Senate Chamber

Thereupon the Members of the House, preceded by the Sergeant at Arms and the Speaker, proceeded to the Senate Chamber.

At 2 o'clock and 35 minutes p m the Members returned, and the House was called to order by the Speaker.

Mr. FITZGERALD. Mr. Speaker, as a further mark of respect to the memory of the late Vice President SHERMAN, I move that the House do now adjourn.

The motion was agreed to; and accordingly (at 2 o'clock and 36 minutes p. m.) the House adjourned until to-morrow, Sunday, February 16, 1913, at 12 o'clock noon.

SUNDAY, *March 2, 1913.*

Mr. FINLEY. Mr. Speaker, I move to take from the Speaker's table Senate concurrent resolution 41, relative to the eulogies on the late Vice President SHERMAN.

The SPEAKER. The Clerk will report the resolution

The Clerk read as follows.

Senate concurrent resolution 41

*Resolved by the Senate (the House of Representatives concurring),* That there shall be printed and bound, under the direction of the Joint Committee on Printing, 14,100 copies of the proceedings and the eulogies delivered in Congress on JAMES SCHOOLCRAFT SHERMAN, late Vice President of the United States, with illustration, of which 4,000 copies shall be for the use of the Senate, 8,000 copies for the use of the House of Representatives, 2,000 copies for the use of the Senators and Representatives of the State of New York, and 100 copies, bound in full morocco, for the use of Mrs James Schoolcraft Sherman: *Provided,* That there shall be included in such publications the proclamation of the President and the proceedings in the Supreme Court of the United States upon the death of Vice President SHERMAN, and an account of the funeral services at Utica, N Y.

The resolution was agreed to.

# PROCEEDINGS IN
## THE SUPREME COURT OF THE UNITED STATES

THURSDAY, *October 31, 1912.*

Present. The Chief Justice, Mr. Justice McKenna, Mr. Justice Holmes, Mr. Justice Day, Mr. Justice Lurton, Mr. Justice Hughes, Mr. Justice Van Devanter, Mr. Justice Lamar, and Mr. Justice Pitney.

Mr. Assistant to the Attorney General Fowler addressed the court as follows:

" May it please the Honorable Court:

" I deeply regret the necessity of performing the sorrowful duty of announcing to this honorable court the death of the Hon. JAMES SCHOOLCRAFT SHERMAN, Vice President of the United States

" Through many years of active and valuable public service, Mr. SHERMAN had attained, independent of the office which he occupied, an enviable position in the hearts of his countrymen   Four years ago he was chosen by the people of his country to the position which he held at the time of his death

" Out of respect deemed to be due so exalted a position in a coordinate branch of the Government, and that this honorable body may join with a bereaved Nation in expressing its sorrow at his untimely death, I move that this court do now adjourn until after the funeral."

The Chief Justice responded

" Mr. Attorney General

" The court hears with sorrow the announcement which you make of the death of the Vice President, and as a token of our participation in the burden of loss which the country has suffered, and out of sympathy with his countrymen, the motion you present is granted, and the court will stand adjourned until Monday next."

Adjourned until Monday next at 12 o'clock.

# Proclamation

## By the Governor of the State of New York

---◆---

STATE OF NEW YORK,
EXECUTIVE CHAMBER

JAMES SCHOOLCRAFT SHERMAN, Vice President of the United States, and for twenty years a Member of the House of Representatives from the State of New York, a patriot and statesman, beloved by all who knew him, and honored and esteemed by the entire citizenship of our country, is dead   The people of the State of New York mourn the loss of one of her most illustrious sons   The qualities which won for JAMES SCHOOLCRAFT SHERMAN a high place among the Nation's statesmen and rulers endeared him to the citizenship of his native State   His untimely demise causes great sadness and deserves sorrowful and appropriate recognition

Now, therefore, it is hereby directed, That as a mark of regard for the distinguished dead the flags upon the capitol and upon all the public buildings of the State, including the armories and arsenals of the National Guard, be displayed at half-mast until and including the day of the funeral, and the citizens of the State for a like period are requested to unite in appropriate tokens of respect

GIVEN under my hand and the privy seal of the State at the capitol, in the city of Albany, this first day of November, in the year of our Lord one thousand nine hundred and twelve

[L  S]

JOHN A  DIX

By the Governor
JOHN A  MASON
*Secretary to the Governor*

# PROCEEDINGS OF
## THE COMMON COUNCIL OF THE CITY OF UTICA, N.Y.

IN COMMON COUNCIL,
*Thursday noon, October 31, 1912*

SPECIAL SESSION

Meeting called for the purpose of taking suitable action upon the death of JAMES SCHOOLCRAFT SHERMAN, Vice President of the United States, which occurred at his home in this city at 9 42 p m, Wednesday, October 30, 1912

President Stetson presiding

Present, all members.

In calling the meeting to order, President Stetson addressed the council as follows:

"The occasion which calls us together at this noon hour is indeed a sad one. As you know, Vice President JAMES S. SHERMAN last evening departed this life.

"While the death of our distinguished citizen, who has so efficiently served his city and the Nation, was not unexpected, yet the news of his passing came as a shock to the community.

"Genuine grief will not pause at the threshold of his home, but will spread itself throughout the entire land

"Mr. SHERMAN was a genial gentleman, who had the faculty of making fast friends of those with whom he came in contact. That he had due regard for those things which are most ennobling in life can be best attested by his achievements as a servant of the people He was a friend to his neighbors, thoughtful of others, unselfish, and courageous.

"Here he was known and loved because he was known, and here his considerate, helpful, and gracious presence will be sorrowfully missed.

"He strove for advancement and attained honorable position as the reward of application. He had earned for himself national distinction and held next to the highest office within the gift of the people of the Nation He was our shining light.

"While he was approaching life's period of whitened locks, he had reached the summit of a remarkable career, in the zenith of his fame, and in his departure we may find consolation in the fact that he was loved and honored and will be mourned by all who knew him and appreciated his worth.

"It is most fitting that this council, in behalf of the people of the city, take appropriate action expressive of the sorrow which his death occasions."

Alderman Dickinson addressed the council as follows.

"Mr. President and Gentlemen This is an occasion when mere words prove but feeble vehicles for the conveyance of the sadness which burdens our hearts. We are mourners at the bier of one we loved. Our admiration for the statesmanship of the Vice President, who lies to-day clothed in the ineffable majesty of death, is shared by 90,000,000 fellow people of the great Republic of which he was an ornament, but our deep and abiding love for our neighbor and friend is a tender and holy sentiment which transcends mere admiration and can be shared only by those nearer ones to whom he was "Jim"—Sunny Jim—personal friend, genial companion, intimate associate.

"In history JAMES SCHOOLCRAFT SHERMAN will be given an elevated place as a constructive statesman, a bulwark of a great political party, a tireless and consistent advocate of certain national policies, and as the most gifted Presiding Officer who ever graced the Senate Chamber.

"Here in Utica his memory will fill a more intimate, more personal chamber in our hearts—a chamber redolent with the fragrance of the flowers of genial fellowship, helpful citizenship, cordial intimacy, and wholesome, tender affection. The ruddy countenance which bespoke the warm red blood pulsating through his arteries, the genial smile which was but a radiation from a generous and humanity-loving heart, the warm handclasp which electrified with the knowledge that back of it was genuine affection, the cheery word before which the pessimism took its flight—these will be cherished in Utica so long as lives any of the thousands who knew and loved JIM SHERMAN—the JIM SHERMAN whose untimely death at the very height of his splendid career has draped our public edifices in black and brought a sense of personal bereavement to our hearts."

Alderman Miller presented the following and asked unanimous consent for an immediate vote thereon, which was granted:

"The common council of the city of Utica assembles in special session to-day to give testimony to its profound sorrow and the sorrow of all our people at the death of JAMES SCHOOLCRAFT SHERMAN

"As mayor of our city for 2 years, as our Representative in Congress for 18 years, and as Vice President of the United States for 4 years, he attained an eminence in public life never before achieved by any other citizen of this community. The honor and prominence which he brought to his native city were sources of pride to his neighbors and friends, no less than a marked distinction to the community and a tribute to his own remarkable personality and splendid attainments  In this city, which saw the beginning of his illustrious career and was the field of his earliest triumphs and whose interests he always held peculiarly his own, his death is felt as a deep and lasting personal loss.

"That he achieved by his own ability and distinguished personality the second highest office in this great Nation, that he was a statesman among statesmen whose honor and integrity were above reproach, whose purposes were ever pure and lofty, who impressed himself upon the history of his country—those things and many more are known to all men.

"But to us, his neighbors and friends, there comes the vivid memory of the genial disposition and beautiful traits of character which endeared him to all, an appreciation of his deep convictions and intensity of purpose in all that he undertook; a knowledge of his utter disregard for caste and his ready recognition of merit and ability, whether in friend or foe, in person of high or low degree  He was a man of boundless energy, of loyal devotion to the measures of public policy which he believed to be for the best interests of the people, and of a beautiful courage, which he displayed at all times, even in the face of the most discouraging opposition.

"With no disposition to intrude upon the grief of his devoted but afflicted family in this sad hour, we feel that as the official representatives of the city—the home which he loved so well and to which he brought such merited distinction—we should tender to them this expression of our heartfelt sympathy and the assurance of our deep appreciation of his splendid public career and his beautiful private life."

Yeas—Aldermen Dickinson, Galligan, Geiersbach, Goldbas, Hirt, Hughes, Kaufer, Miller, Nicholson, Pellettieri, Pugh, Redmond, Ryan, Simmonds, Weikert—15

Nays—None.

Adopted

By Alderman GOLDBAS:

*Resolved,* That the City Hall be draped in mourning, the flags on all public buildings lowered to half-mast for a period of 30 days, and that all public offices of the city be closed during the hours of the funeral of Vice President SHERMAN, as an official tribute of respect to his memory.

Yeas—Aldermen Dickinson, Galligan, Geiersbach, Goldbas, Hirt, Hughes, Kaufer, Miller, Nicholson, Pellettieri, Pugh, Redmond, Ryan, Simmonds, Weikert—15.

Nays—None.

Adopted.

Adjourned

J. P BANNIGAN,
*City Clerk.*

In Common Council,
*Friday evening, November 1, 1912.*

President Stetson presiding

Present. All members, except Aldermen Miller, Pellettieri, and Ryan.

By Alderman Hughes:

*Resolved,* That as a mark of respect to the memory of our late esteemed fellow townsman, James Schoolcraft Sherman, Vice President of the United States, the common council does hereby request that all business of every kind and description in this city cease during the hours of his funeral from 2 to 4 p. m. to-morrow.

Adopted.

By Alderman Dickinson:

*Resolved,* That the common council of the city of Utica hereby determines to attend in a body the funeral of our deceased esteemed fellow citizen, James Schoolcraft Sherman, Vice President of the United States, meeting for this purpose at Hotel Utica at 1.30 p m. to-morrow, and that out of respect to his revered memory this council does now adjourn.

Adopted.

Adjourned.

J. P. Bannigan,
*City Clerk*

## PROCLAMATION BY THE MAYOR OF THE CITY OF UTICA, N Y.

*To the citizens of Utica*

As a final tribute to the memory of Utica's illustrious son, Hon James S. Sherman, Vice President of the United States, I would respectfully urge that all business be suspended throughout the city between the hours of 1 and 4 o'clock on Saturday.

The funeral services of the Vice President will be held at the First Presbyterian Church at 2 o'clock. Many business houses will close during the afternoon, while operations will be suspended in many manufacturing establishments. I would respectfully request a complete cessation of business during the hours of the funeral services

Frank J. Baker, *Mayor.*

Utica, N. Y., *November 1, 1912.*

# PROCEEDINGS OF THE PHILIPPINE GOVERNMENT

[Governor General's proclamation.]

EXECUTIVE ORDER }
No. 76.

THE GOVERNMENT OF THE PHILIPPINE ISLANDS,
EXECUTIVE BUREAU,
*Manila, November 2, 1912.*

The announcement of the death of the Hon JAMES SCHOOLCRAFT SHERMAN, Vice President of the United States, has been received with sincere and general sorrow. Since the beginning of his public career he has steadily grown in the estimation of the American people, and his distinguished ability and service have been universally recognized

It is deemed fitting that the deep grief which fills all hearts should find formal expression. Therefore, the President of the United States has directed that the flags on all Government buildings be placed at half-staff from sunrise until sunset to-day, November second It is further ordered that all public business in the various offices of this Government be suspended so far as practicable during the same period.

NEWTON W. GILBERT,
*Acting Governor General.*

---

PHILIPPINE LEGISLATURE EXPRESSES SORROW

On the day of Vice President SHERMAN's funeral, November 2, 1912, the third Philippine Legislature adopted the following resolution and adjourned in respect to his memory:

" JOINT RESOLUTION Expressing the grief of both houses of the legislature on account of the death of the Hon JAMES SCHOOLCRAFT SHERMAN, Vice President of the United States, and providing for the adjournment of both houses as a token of sorrow

"*Resolved by the Philippine Commission and the Philippine Assembly,* That they express, as they hereby do express, the profound sorrow with which they have received the announcement of the death of the Hon. JAMES SCHOOLCRAFT SHERMAN, Vice President of the United States,

"*Resolved further,* That the session of both houses be, and hereby is, immediately adjourned in token of their sorrow for this day;

[89]

"*And resolved further,* That the secretary of the Philippine Commission or the secretary of the Philippine Assembly shall furnish a certified copy of this resolution to the President of the United States, through the chief executive of the Philippines, and to the family of the deceased"

### NARVACAN COUNCIL MANIFESTS REGRET

The municipal council of Narvacan, Province of Ilocos Sur, P. I., at the suggestion of the president, Mr Pedro Viloria Bañez, and on motion of Mr. Poinciano Viloria, seconded by the vice president, Mr. Aniceto Corrales, adopted the following resolution on November 27, 1912·

"*Resolved,* To express, and it hereby does express, the fact that it has received with profound regret the notice regarding the death of the Hon. James Schoolcraft Sherman, Vice President of the United States.

"*Resolved, further,* That the municipal secretary be directed to forward, through his excellency, the governor general of the Philippine Islands, certified copies hereof, not only to His Excellency, the President of the United States, but also to the family of the deceased."

# FUNERAL SERVICES

[From the Utica (N Y ) Daily Press, Nov. 2, 1912 ]

FRIENDS GET FINAL GLIMPSE—THOUSANDS GAZE SORROWFULLY—BODY
OF VICE PRESIDENT LIES AT THE COUNTY BUILDING, WHERE FOR
HOURS MEMBERS OF GRIEVED COMMUNITY PASS FOR LAST LOOK ON
HIS FACE—IMPRESSIVE AND SOLEMN EXERCISES.

The body of Vice President SHERMAN was placed in state in the
courthouse in this city yesterday afternoon and remained on
view until well into the night, and during these hours was seen
by many thousands.  There were no formal exercises, but the
proceedings were conducted in a quiet, dignified manner befit-
ting the solemnity of the occasion.  About a thousand of Mr
SHERMAN's neighbors and friends marched in the procession
which acted as escort  Chairman Thomas R Proctor and members of the reception committee were inside the house.  The
veterans of the Grand Army of the Republic, led by Maj. James
Miller and E. C. Ferry, were ranged on both sides of the south
walk.  It was about 2.30 p. m  when the hearse drew up at the
curb and the procession began forming  All heads were uncovered as the body was brought to the door.  The members of the
Boosters' committee were ranged each side of the hearse and
the members of the reception committee, headed by Rev. Louis
H. Holden, Ph. D., escorted the remains from the house to the
hearse.  The procession started for the courthouse in the fol-
lowing order·
Platoon of police headed by Officer McCarthy, who was Mr.
SHERMAN's bodyguard in 1908.
Veterans of the Civil War led by Maj. James Miller and E. C.
Ferry, Capt Frank S Judson of the Cavalry troop acting as
marshal.
Utica Lodge Benevolent Protective Order of Elks, 300 men.
Hearse.
Business men's escort, William H. Roberts, F. X. Matt, Russell
Wheeler, William E Richards, Hon. Henry Martin, Oscar S.
Foster, William E Lewis, M Jesse Brayton, Charles W. Wicks,
F. M. Kendrick, D. D. Smythe, A H. Munson, Patrick J McQuade,
E. J. Millspaugh, F A. Bosworth, Lieut. W. G. Mayer, John L.
Maher, George B. Allen, B Allen Whiffen, James H. Gilmore, John
A Cantwell, Wilbur S. Clark, Charles Millar, Brian Clarke, Messrs
Jefferson, Safford, DeLong, and others.

[91]

Reception committee, Thomas R. Proctor, chairman, Robert Fraser, George L. Bradford, W. S. Doolittle, Frederick T. Proctor, Charles A. Miller, Charles B. Rogers, George E. Dunham, J. Fred Maynard, William T. Baker, Hon F. M. Calder, Hon. John D Kernan, Perle W Harter, Edgar B. Odell, Otto A. Meyer, Hon P C. J. DeAngelis, Hon Charles S Symonds

Automobile containing Dr Holden, Sherrill Babcock, and others. City officials, bankers, and business men generally

Prof. Emidio Spina and Vincenzo Marrone, of La Luce, in which Mr. SHERMAN was a stockholder.

Utica Republican Club, over 100 members

As the procession moved slowly down Genesee Street it was viewed by thousands standing on the sidewalks. Nearly all the dwellings and places of business displayed the Stars and Stripes at half-mast and bound with crêpe. While the procession was en route, the city hall bell was tolled

The courthouse was profusely draped in mourning. In the center of the rotunda directly opposite the entrance on the main floor a catafalque had been made of flags, and above this was a canopy formed of large flags. At the right and left were screens formed of palms Near by on benches were large wreaths of orchids, roses, carnations, and Easter lilies

Capt. Peter Arheilger had charge of the police outside, and at the entrances and inside were about 50 members of the National Guard, Companies A and B, in charge of Lieut. E K. Miller and Lieut Chester W Davis Two soldiers stood at the head and two at the foot, and they were frequently relieved.

The body was incased in a massive casket of mahogany covered with black broadcloth and having massive bar extension handles of antique silver. On the casket was a large cross of white lilies fringed with maidenhair fern. Mr SHERMAN's face was placid and serene, and his position was natural Those who made up the escorting column were the first to look at the remains. As the members of the Elks passed through each took from his buttonhole an ivy leaf and placed it on the casket

There was no music, no display, no speeches, but as a resident and former mayor of Utica and as Vice President of the United States, Mr. SHERMAN belonged to the people, and their desire to see his face again before it should be lost to sight was natural and sincere. To place the body in a public building in a place easy of access, where people could see it conveniently, was a courtesy on the part of his family which was highly appreciated. The spectators entered by the front door, formed in two lines, and with uncovered heads and measured tread they proceeded to the bier, where they paused for an instant and took a last look and a mental farewell of the sleeper, and then passed on and out of the door just opposite. It was done quietly and reverently and in less time than it takes to write it. It was silent, yet eloquent, a simple yet beautiful demonstration dictated by a feeling of friendship for the dead and sympathy for his surviving relatives.

Never was there a better opportunity to study the composite character of the population of Utica than by watching the crowd which passed through the courthouse in viewing the remains of Mr. SHERMAN  For the first hour or two women and school children were in the majority.  Among those in this period were clergymen, school-teachers, lawyers, and doctors.  After 5 o'clock there were more men, and from 5.30 to 6 30 there were mostly men  Then there was a falling off for about an hour, but shortly after 7 o'clock the crowd began to increase, and soon there was a jam outside the building, so that people were obliged to stand in line for from 15 to 20 minutes until they could get inside.  Once inside they made speedy progress, for the soldiers had things well systematized and kept the line moving  From 7 to 8 o'clock the crowd was large, and passed through at the rate of 5,000 an hour.  The spectators were not confined to Uticans, but there were delegations from nearly every town in the county and some from Herkimer County

The evening crowd comprised mostly the men and women who were at work during the day in all sorts of occupations. And, though they were of all ages, colors, nationalities, and races, all showed that they felt the presence of death and knew the kinship of sorrow.  A delegation of about 50 boys from St Vincent Industrial School viewed the remains about 5 30.  They were accompanied by Brother Director Gregory

Just before the doors were closed the members of Utica Council, Knights of Columbus, passed through in a body.  They were led by Knight McCreary and numbered about 200.  The Sherman Boosters came in just after 9 o'clock.

At about 9 30 the remains were carried out the Mary Street entrance to the hearse  The members of Companies A and B of the National Guard acted as escort, and formed on either side of the hearse.  The Elks, Boosters, and members of the Republican Club also joined the column and accompanied the remains up Genesee Street back to the home of Mr SHERMAN.  When the body was taken to and from the city hall all street cars en route were stopped as a mark of respect to Mr SHERMAN, who was an officer in the company.

A large wreath presented by the Boosters rested at the side of the casket and a magnificent wreath of orchids from former Congressman Littauer was close by.

The Elks acted as escort, at the request of the family of Mr SHERMAN.  Mr SHERMAN had an Elks badge in the lapel of his coat.

Rev. Louis H. Holden, Ph. D., read appropriate prayers at the home of Mr SHERMAN yesterday afternoon before the remains were taken to the courthouse.

[From the Utica (N Y) Daily Press, Nov. 4, 1912 ]

MR SHERMAN AT REST—FUNERAL NOTABLE FOR ITS PROPORTION AND
DISTINCTION—A NATIONAL AND CIVIC EVENT—DIGNITARIES OF
STATE, INCLUDING THE PRESIDENT OF THE REPUBLIC, UNITE WITH
NEIGHBORS AND FRIENDS IN THE LAST TRIBUTE OF RESPECT.

The funeral of Hon. JAMES S. SHERMAN, Vice President of the
United States and Utica's foremost citizen, was held from the
First Presbyterian Church of this city at 2 o'clock Saturday afternoon. In size and proportion it was the largest ever held in this
city. Those who attended the services at the church, although
they filled the edifice, were but a fragment as compared with the
throng that filled the streets and which was none the less ardent
in its devotion to the eminent dead, or less willing to pay formal
tribute if given opportunity It is estimated that there were
25,000 persons in the streets of Utica on this sorrowful day.

In distinction, likewise, no such funeral has ever before been
held in Utica. The President of the United States, in the person
of Mr Taft, justices of the Supreme Court, United States Senators,
Representatives in Congress, and State dignitaries from all parts
of the country were in attendance. Men famed in various walks
of life, friends of the departed, were also present

The people of Utica never paid a more universal and more
heartfelt tribute at the bier of any of its sons. The city paused
in its various activities to do honor to the man who had done so
much for it in life and brought it distinction even in death.

The rumble of traffic was hushed as the city-hall bell tolled the
approaching hour of the obsequies. Simultaneously flags were at
half-mast in every State in the Union and in all the possessions
of the Government, to the remotest and smallest island Public
buildings were closed and from every warship a salute of 19
minute guns was fired, echoing around the world, while every
officer of the Army, Navy, and Marine Corps wore an emblem of
mourning

No other Utican has ever received such a testimonial of honor
and respect Nation and city united in the tribute. The grief of
the many mourners, friends, and kindred will be assuaged, in a
measure, by the thought that the character and position of the
departed were such as to command the praise and homage of a
whole people.

The services at the church were simple in form, yet solemn
and impressive They partook somewhat of the quality of
majesty. No services conducted in such presence could fail to
give such an impression. There were seated many of the governing minds of a mighty nation as well as representatives of
the highest culture—chiefs of state, of business, and education.

President Stryker of Hamilton College delivered a touching and
feeling eulogy. It was the sincere tribute of a friend to a friend
who had gone hither. Without show or ostentation, he told of

the excellent qualities of the departed and the blessings and certainty of immortality. President Taft looked directly at the speaker throughout the discourse, and was evidently deeply impressed. His attitude was typical of the attitude of all  The speaker communicated his emotion to the assemblage, and there were many tear-stained eyes.

Sympathy radiated to the gentle and broken widow, the bereaved sons, and other kindred.

The perfume of the beautiful flowers, like incense, pervaded the atmosphere of the auditorium.  The black and purple of the mourning emblems gave a somber touch and color wholly in keeping with the sorrowful occasion.  The music was attuned with the universal feeling

Outside was the crowd, not sharing in the inspiration of eulogy, music, and incense, but none the less solemn and reverent.

The procession was formed and slowly wended its way between two files of bowed humanity to the cemetery, where the final rites of the funeral were performed, the last adieu said by the family, and the body of JAMES SCHOOLCRAFT SHERMAN laid at rest

WITH THOSE WHO LOOKED ON—VAST CROWDS THRONGED THE STREETS—PROCESSIONS TO AND FROM CHURCH.

Gray clouds racing low across cold windswept sky, a piercing chill that cut to the marrow, and a few light flakes of snow drifting downward—these formed a fit setting of dreariness and sorrow to the final rites accorded to JAMES SCHOOLCRAFT SHERMAN Saturday afternoon, when Utica and the surrounding towns poured thousands of spectators into the center of the city and along the route of the funeral procession.

It had been announced in the papers that certain portions of the First Presbyterian Church not occupied by those entitled to reserved seats would be opened to the public, and long before 11 o'clock the crowds began to gather outside the building where the public funeral services were to be held

The distinguished visitors of national reputation headed the procession which was formed in the Hotel Utica lobby and the Italian room  Members of the Republican Club of the city, together with the executive officers of the city, followed next in line  The clergy, the common council, and the members of the consistory of Christ Church completed the procession to the church which was formed at the hotel

It was 2 20 o'clock when the tolling of the city hall bell announced that the funeral cortège had left the Sherman home, following the services there.  The big bell tolled solemnly on with momentary intervals until after the procession reached the church.

When the body was placed in the hearse the carriages were filled as follows:

1. Mrs Sherman and Sherrill Sherman.
2. Mr. and Mrs. Richard U. Sherman, Mr. and Mrs. Thomas M. Sherman
3. Mrs Sherrill Sherman, Mrs L. B Moore, Capt Babcock, Mr. Littauer.
4. Mrs William B Jackson, Mr and Mrs. H. J. Cookinham, Mrs. Rice.
5. Mr. and Mrs. Richard W. Sherman, Miss Bessie Sherman, Mrs. Dick.
6. Mr and Mrs. Sanford Sherman, Mr and Mrs. Alfred Hatfield
7. Mr and Mrs. James De Long, the Misses De Long
8. Mr. and Mrs. H. J. Cookinham, jr, Mr. and Mrs. Frederick Cookinham.
9. Mr and Mrs. Edward Cookinham, Mr and Mrs. Henry H. Cooper, jr.
10. Walter Cookinham, Robert Sherman, the Misses Rice.
11. Judge and Mrs. Alfred C. Coxe, Mr and Mrs. Julius Doolittle.
12. Miss Isabel Doolittle, Mr. and Mrs. W. C. J. Doolittle.
13. Mr and Mrs. Brian Clark, Mrs Roberts
14. Mr and Mrs Charles H Childs, Miss Nellie Barber.
15. Thomas Baker, the Misses Baker, Miss Connelly.
16. Hon and Mrs. George Fairchild, Hon. L W. Emerson.

There were in all 42 carriages at the Sherman home, and the greater share of the remainder were filled without regard to special order  The procession then moved toward the church, preceded by the honorary and active bearers

At 2.34 the carriage containing Dr Stryker, Dr. Holden, and Dr. Brokaw arrived at the entrance of the church.

Then the bearers arrived, followed by the hearse.  The heavy casket, covered with flowers and containing the body of Utica's distinguished son, was lifted reverently from the hearse and carried up the steps of the church.

The arrival of Mrs Sherman was the signal for a general silent manifestation of sympathy.  Everywhere hats were lifted and quiet murmurs of sympathy came from the women.  Mrs. Sherman was escorted to the church by her sons, Richard and Sherrill.

When the distinguished visitors and those having cards of admission were seated such of the public as could be seated in the remaining space were admitted.  While the service was in progress the throng about the church and up Washington Street could easily stand an estimate of 18,000.  The crowd immediately about the church extended over Columbia Street and down Washington Street to Lafayette

After the services, the general public was admitted through the chapel doors of the church to view the flowers and decorations

Between the double line of Senators, Congressmen, and Justices of the Supreme Court the casket was borne to the hearse and the flowers placed upon it. The immediate family and President Taft and suite followed, and the procession took up the line of march to the cemetery.

Up Washington Street to Genesee the 42 carriages moved in slow time between thousands of spectators that lined both sides of the route as far as Court Street. From there on the spectators were on the west side of the street and four deep as far as South Street. Every corner was crowded, and at Oneida Square another crowd awaited the cortège.

At 3 45 o'clock the body of the dead Vice President passed the Sherman home for the last time. The house stood dark and grim in the failing light of the afternoon as the master of the house passed on forever. No crowd assembled there, but from the windows of the near-by homes faces looked out to see the last of their good friend and neighbor. The march continued past the House of the Good Shepherd, where the waiting lines of orphans bowed their heads in respect to the passing hearse

Following out the suggestion made by Mayor Baker in his proclamation Saturday morning, the business houses of the city closed their doors from 2 o'clock until 4. The national colors, tied with crêpe or black and purple bunting, appeared all along the line of march, and the business section of the city presented a Sunday afternoon appearance.

In compliance with orders issued yesterday, all electric cars in the city stopped at 2 o'clock and remained stationary for five minutes The business offices of the railway company were closed all day. It was in these ways that the local electric company expressed the sympathy due to a distinguished citizen and a stockholder in the company

---

SERVICES AT THE HOME—ONLY RELATIVES AND A VERY FEW FRIENDS GATHER THERE BEFORE THE PUBLIC CHURCH SERVICE.

Intimate, and because of that intimacy the more sorrowful, were the services conducted Saturday afternoon at the home of Vice President SHERMAN. There gathered the members of his family and a few very close friends who were given this opportunity to pay their tribute of honor and affection to the man they had known and loved. It was for this reason that the services took on an aspect essentially private, although President Taft was present for part of the service.

The casket containing the body of Vice President SHERMAN was placed in the parlor at the north side of the house. In that room were seats for some of the family and the President's party, while other seats were placed in the hall and the adjoining rooms. The honorary bearers, who were Senator Elihu Root, Thomas R. Proctor, Charles S. Symonds, William S. Doolittle, J Francis Day, George E Dunham, Charles B. Rogers, William T Baker, Henry H. Cooper, and Dr Fayette H Peck, were seated in a room at the rear of the hall until such time as they were called to perform the duties of their sad office   Near them also were waiting the active bearers from the Utica Trust & Deposit Co., of which Mr SHERMAN was president: Graham Coventry, Charles J. Lamb, Grover C. Clark, George W. Williams, Floyd E. Ecker, H R. Huntington, C. R. Hicks, H. P. Thomas, J C. Cody, R E. Roberts.

Everywhere were to be seen the beautiful flowers which had been sent to express the sympathy of friends.  The parlor was banked on every side with these and in the other rooms, too, they were found in profusion.  From persons high and low throughout the country these messengers came, bearing the sympathy of friends who mourned together in the loss of their common friend.

The service had been announced for 1 o'clock, but it was considerably after that before Rev. Louis H Holden, Ph D , pastor of Christ Church, began the Scripture reading.  This he did after President Taft and his party arrived.  They came about 1 40, the President being met by Lieut. W. G Mayer, Thomas R. Proctor, W. S. Doolittle, and others   All stood while the President passed into the parlor to take his place near the body of his dead associate.

After the minister had repeated the Twenty-third Psalm all present joined in reciting the Apostles' Creed.  Then they were seated while Dr Holden read the Scriptures, his selections being taken from I Corinthians xv and John xiv.  He offered a brief prayer, ending with the Lord's Prayer.  Then followed the benediction

The singing, which was under the direction of Dr. F. P. Cavallo, was beautiful and lent much to the dignity and impressiveness of the occasion.  The Schubert quartet, composed of Mrs Hugh T. Owen, soprano, Mrs. Lelia Ryan Schilz, contralto; Dr. Cavallo, bass, and Elliott H Stewart, tenor, sang " Paradise, Oh Paradise " and "Rock of Ages."  There was also a male quartet, composed of Mr. Stewart, first tenor, Thomas E Ryan, second tenor; A Spencer Hughes, first bass, and Dr. Cavallo, second bass.  They sang an arrangement of " Crossing the Bar."

While the singing was in progress the bearers had left the home with their sad burden, and already the hearse was moving slowly down Genesee Street at the head of a mournful procession.  As fast as the carriages were filled with the members of the family, they joined the slow-moving line which passed between crowds all the way to the church where the public service was held.

INSIDE THE CHURCH—PRESIDENT STRYKER OF HAMILTON COLLEGE
PAYS AFFECTING TRIBUTE TO MEMORY OF A DEAR FRIEND

The church doors were not open till just before the hour of
the funeral, but the ushers were on hand as early as 1 o'clock.
They were: From the Conkling Unconditionals, Arthur J. Lowery,
chief, Spencer Kellogg, Frank B. Rathbun, Edward B. Ibbotson,
Charles DeAngelis, Russell Brennan, William A. Clark, Edward
K. Miller, Chester W. Davis, Bradford C. Divine, Frederick W.
Kincaid, A. C. Brinckerhoff, Fred B Adams, Stewart Snyder,
M. Angelo Cooper, Rex Witherbee, George Ladue, Charles L.
Williams, from the First Presbyterian Church, Dr F. H Brewer,
Dr. E. D Fuller, J. C. Hamilton.

The interior of the church was profusely draped with emblems
of mourning. The base was black and the overdrapings of
purple. The reredos was covered with black and purple and
at the sides were festoons of similar hues. The gallery front
was covered with black and overdrapings of purple, and festoons
of the same colors were under each window. The columns were
wound, and the front pews, occupied by the President and by
Mrs. Sherman, were covered with black and a large flag.

The floral tributes were the most numerous and costly ever
seen at a funeral in this city. They filled the chancel and the
space in front. In the center was a large flag in flowers, the
gift of the Utica Republican Club. On one side of the pulpit
was a large cross from the Conkling Unconditionals and on the
other a large cross of white chrysanthemums trimmed with
orchids from the officials at the city hall. Other pieces were
a wreath of orchids from the United States Senate, a wreath of
white roses from the House of Representatives, and beautiful
floral pieces from the Secretary of State and Mrs. Knox, the minister of Salvador, the Dominican Republic, the Guatemalan minister and Señora Doña Luz Méndez, the German ambassador and
Countess Bernstorff, the National Republican League, the American Protective Tariff League, the Republican city and county
committee, Charles V. Schram, large cross with "Auld Lang Syne"
in flowers from the Hebrew people of Utica, a large wreath of
white flowers on palms by Harry Gerber and Samuel Stone. On
this was a card inscribed, "For He will give His angels charge
concerning thee, to guard thee in all thy ways." Large floral
piece from Herkimer County friends  Other floral pieces were
from Minard J Fisher, Miss Florence Millar, and Charles Millar, a
blanket of chrysanthemums from the congregation of Christ
Church.

At 1 30 the doors to the galleries were opened and the galleries
were at once filled. Next the side aisles were opened and filled
almost as quickly  At 1 50 the congressional party entered, then
the Justices of the Supreme Court and the trustees of Hamilton

College  The Conkling Unconditionals were seated in the chancel. When President Taft, former Vice President Fairbanks, and the other officers entered, the audience rose and remained standing until the President was seated.

The President occupied a seat in the center aisle of the church, and with him sat Attorney General Wickersham, Secretary Nagel, of the Department of Commerce and Labor, former Vice President Fairbanks, and Chairman Hilles, of the Republican national committee.

Immediately back of them were seated Justices Hughes and Pitney, of the United States Supreme Court, Senators Crane, Curtis, Lippitt, Penrose, Oliver, Bacon, Works, and O'Gorman; Secretary Bennett, of the Senate, and Representatives Dalzell, Calder, Jones, Wright, Fairchild, Fitzgerald, Dwight, Knapp, Cocks, and other Members of the National House of Representatives.  Senator Root was seated with the honorary pallbearers.

Others in the assemblage included former Govs. Frank S. Black and Benjamin B Odell, jr., and members of the New York State Legislature.  Gov. Dix was unable to be present, but sent Lieut. Commander Eckford C DeKay, his military secretary, as his representative

The casket, covered with violets and lilies of the valley, was borne into the church at 2 30 o'clock, and following it came Mrs. Sherman in heavy mourning, leaning on the arm of her son Sherrill.  She was accompanied by other members of the Sherman family.  All were given seats in close proximity to the casket. The Mendelssohn funeral march was played as the body was carried in and deposited immediately in front of the altar.

The entire audience arose in silence as the bearers made their way to the front.  First came the honorary bearers and the active bearers with the remains and then the members of the family and relatives.  The Republican Club occupied the chapel in rear of the pulpit

The music was in charge of Charles W. Mowry, organist and choir master.  While the pews were filling the organ played the following selections·  "Adagio and Andante"; C Minor Sonata, Mendelssohn, Elegy, Halsey, Largo, Handel, Legend, Foulkes

The choir was made up of the following  Sopranos, Miss Carmelita Wilkes, Miss Florence Lumley, Mrs. Hugh T Owen, altos, Miss Calista Gardner, Miss Florence Debbold, Mrs Leila Ryan Schilz, tenors, Thomas G. Jones, Alfred Jay, and Elliott H. Stewart, bassos, Herbert Jones, A. Spencer Hughes, Hugh T. Owen

The services opened with the choir singing " Lead, Kindly Light."  Rev. Louis H Holden, Ph D , read passages of Scripture which declare the blessed assurance of eternal life

### PRESIDENT STRYKER'S ADDRESS

The address by President M. Woolsey Stryker, of Hamilton College, was brief but full of feeling. Dr Stryker never spoke more deliberately, and when he came to say the words of farewell he looked down from the pulpit on the form of Mr. SHERMAN below and his voice choked with emotion. Many in the audience were moved to tears. Dr Stryker spoke as follows:

"In solemn and united mourning, but with tearful gratitude and calm, reasonable hope, we are met in this house of faith to remember him whose form is before us in all the mysterious dignity and the eloquent silence of death. We represent, while we deeply share, a general public sorrow. The high representatives of State and Nation assemble with us, who are his neighbors, in keen human sympathy, to make a common tribute of manly regard and manly affection to an exalted dignitary of the land and to an endeared companion. We lament the passing, not first of the Vice President of the United States, but of JAMES SCHOOLCRAFT SHERMAN, the man. This community shares in these acts of devotion, aware that there is gone their preeminent—long-time such—preeminent fellow citizen, but also that one is gone whose cordial courtesy and whose indomitable and impartial kindliness made him the counselor and the helper of innumerable men.

"In the name of you all, I assure this household of your keen and profound heed for their distress, and in their names I thank you for your presence and for that swift telepathy in which you identify your grief with theirs. You put out to them warm and firm hands and they take them gladly, and unspeakably they thank you.

"I speak for that college circle which had delight and honor in this elect and loyal comrade and for those, its trustees, whose labors he zealously shared. And I speak—alas, that words are so poor!—as an intimate and sorrowing friend, one of many, so many who grieve that we shall here not see him any more. Not even with the most urgent brevity may I at all recite his consistent and influential career. No, nor his earthly honors. No, nor his noble traits. All these are legible; written past recall. Our hearts review them. Nor will we ever forget. Least of all may I lead you, with steps however soft, into the sanctities of that domestic love which are his endearing legacies. We intermeddle not with that joy

"Good-by, good and faithful servant, great heart, gentle friend, good-by. Here be it remembered that this man was one whose patience and whose courage drank deep of that spiritual rock. Never was he ashamed of his hope in the Master of Life, whom ever since long ago he quietly and steadfastly confessed before men.

[101]

"Yes, farewell  Let the mortal put on immortality.  We, the pilgrims of the night who still dwell in tents, salute thee in thy secure abode where all shadows are swallowed up of day. Thanks be to God for every good fight fought through, for every victory won through pain; for Him, the Captain of the Cross, who leads steadily His own to where, beyond these voices, there is peace."

At the conclusion of his address, Dr. Stryker proceeded at once with his prayer, in which he said:

"Therefore, Almighty and Merciful God, we bow before Thee and acknowledge Thy sovereign will in us.  Come death, come life, we lay in Thy hand the secure keeping the dear dust of the dead.  We remember with joy and gratitude before Thee all wherein Thy life touched theirs with beauty and with power. We pray that we may so follow the good example of those who sleep in Jesus Christ that, after this painful life is ended, we may dwell with Thee in life everlasting.  Thou Who didst with Thine own lips say, 'I will not leave you orphans, I will care for you with more than human love,' dost regard these friends of ours in their sorrow  Let there be light in their dwellings  Let the peace of God that passeth all understanding guard their hearts and their thoughts in Christ.  Make us all, O God, more tender and more true by this day's experience.  Let our vows be registered with Thee while our hearts praise Thy name.  Join us with the blessed company of those everywhere who trust and serve and bow and wait  And in Thy due time, through Thy great mercy, through Jesus Christ, who won for all, receive us into everlasting habitations.  Thou who hast said, 'Because I live, ye shall live also,' we do not ask that the way of life may be made soft and easy to our feet, but we ask that it may be made plain.  Help us to bear the day's burden, to endure the trials of the instant  We leave all things in Thy good hands and do commit ourselves and all this presence to Thy faithful care, and, when this is over, open to us Thy door that at last we may know Thee whom we have so much forgotten, and know as we are known.

"Thou that takest away the sins of the world, have mercy on us.  Thou that takest away the sins of the world, grant us Thy peace.  Amen."

Then, at the request of President Stryker, the audience rose and joined the choir in singing with great earnestness the well-known hymn, "Nearer, My God, to Thee."  It was the first time that those in the congregation had had an opportunity to give expression to their feelings, and they sang the five verses of the hymn with an earnestness seldom heard  President Taft sang as fervently as any, as did President Stryker

The benediction was announced by the pastor of the church, Rev. Ralph W. Brokaw, D. D  The choir sang with fine expression the well-known prayer hymn, "Abide with Me," after which the remains were borne from the church, the funeral procession being made up of the honorary bearers, clergy, the remains, members of the family and mourners, President Taft, and the other officials in their order. For a recessional the organ played Mendelssohn's funeral march.

The official position of Mr. Taft, as President of the United States, entitled him to ride ahead of the hearse, but he preferred to be a mourner, and at his own request was given a place behind Mr. SHERMAN's immediate family

The floral tributes were so numerous that they could not all be brought into the church, but all were taken to the cemetery. Among them were wreaths and other designs from the following· Mr and Mrs. S C Neale, J. G Small and wife, National Republican League, Mr. and Mrs. Albert Hatfield, Mr. and Mrs. C. H Poole, employees of the Utica Trust & Deposit Co., Hon. and Mrs. M E. Driscoll, Beta Chapter of the Sigma Phi fraternity, Hon. J. W. Weeks, Republican county and city committee, Mr and Mrs. O H Hammond, Mr. and Mrs F. M Peckham, Mr. and Mrs. D. H. Hazard, Hon Charles L. Knapp, Mr. and Mrs George E Dunham, William H Hawk and daughter, Mr. and Mrs. R. A. C. Smith, Mr. and Mrs. J C. Bishop, the Northern New York Trust Co., Hon. L N Littauer, Judge W B. Hooker and family, the Spanish minister, the minister of Haiti, the Secretary of State and Mrs. Knox, Hon. F. M. Davenport, the United States Senate, George W. Hinman, Mr. and Mrs. Brian Clarke, and employees of the Utica post office.

A magnificent wreath from President and Mrs. Taft did not arrive till late, but Mrs. Sherman, accompanied by members of her family, went to the cemetery and placed it in the mausoleum yesterday morning

---

AT THE CEMETERY—HUNDREDS GATHER TO WATCH THE FINAL SERVICES AS VICE PRESIDENT SHERMAN IS LAID TO REST.

The scene at the committal service in Forest Hill Cemetery was one never to be forgotten. There were gathered as closely as they could be grouped the high and low of the earth, for many of the people who are generally described as just "plain folks" were almost rubbing elbows with the President of the United States. And all about them were the resting places of those who are asleep in the last long rest which obliterates all distinctions of place and power.

As sharp as were the contrasts in humanity gathered there, even more sharp were the visible aspects of nature Underfoot along the edges of the drive rustled the dead leaves which had fallen from the many trees Stark and bare the limbs of the trees stood in naked outline against the cold November sky. And yet, grouped

[103]

near the place where the last words of farewell were said in honor of him who is gone, appeared every sort of tribute from the art and skill of the florist. The most beautiful and fragrant forms in which nature displays its floral riches were gathered there in a profusion of color and design  Wonderful wreaths and designs, huge bouquets of lilies, orchids, roses, and violets gave mute testimony of the place in the hearts of his friends which Mr SHERMAN held  These were the tributes of friends who chose in this beautiful manner to express their sympathy. And so these flowers became the eloquent messengers of those whose hearts were perhaps too full to say the things that the flowers meant.

In front of the Babcock-Moore mausoleum a tent had been erected to shelter those who were to take part in the final service. Against the ropes in front crowded hundreds of people, eager to see and yet respectful and reverent, fully appreciating the sadness of the occasion.

About 4 o'clock came a few carriages, bearing more of the flowers which had been brought from the church  There followed a few busy moments arranging these, and then fell the hush of expectancy  Soon the Haydns, numbering about 60, arrived, and they were grouped against the ropes at one side of the plot, to take their share in the service.  Then Dr. M Woolsey Stryker, Dr. Ralph W. Brokaw, and Dr. Louis H Holden arrived.  They were followed by the honorary bearers, who were grouped about the place prepared for the casket before it was finally laid to rest in the crypt

When the hearse stopped before the approach to the mausoleum, the bearers stood near to receive their sad burden  Reverently the crowd uncovered as the men moved slowly away, bearing between them the heavy black symbol of grief.  On top of the casket lay two crosses, one of white lilies and the other of violets, tributes of the family.

The casket was placed on the rests and there was a moment's hush as President Taft, former Vice President Fairbanks, and several others high in the Nation's councils, gathered there for the last tribute of respect and affection.  Meanwhile the Haydns had been singing "Asleep in Jesus" on the tune "Rest," this being at the request of Mrs Sherman  It was the same hymn they had sung at the funeral of Mrs. Sherman's mother not long before.

Dr. Stryker began the committal service, speaking in a low tone, yet so distinctly that his words were heard by many in the crowd.  The reading occupied about three minutes and then the Schubert quartet sang "Good Night."  There followed a moment's stir as President Taft and his party had to take leave. They stepped slowly from the shelter of the tent, to make their way toward the waiting automobiles.  As they left, Richard U. Sherman followed them, to climb into the President's car, shake his hand, and thank him, apparently, for his presence at the funeral.

Reverently the honorary bearers and others who had been a part of the gathering left the tent   There remained but the members of the family, and none wished to intrude on the sacredness of those last moments.  To the relatives belonged the intimacy of the final farewell and no person would have had it otherwise. After the Haydns had sung " Nearer, My God, to Thee," and Dr. Stryker had pronounced the benediction, the service was at an end   Gently the casket was slid into the crypt prepared for it, slowly the crowd turned away to pass quietly down the winding paths

Dusk was giving way to darkness before the last persons had left.  Lights flashing here and there in the valley below picked out the busy places in the city's activity   From afar came a steady impersonal hum as though of many voices talking—in fact, it was the voice of the city   And there through the trees on the hillside whispered the cold November wind.  But it held no terrors for him who was left there asleep—close to the city and people he loved and served so well

---

## MEMORIAL SERVICES IN BERLIN

A memorial service in honor of the late Vice President JAMES SCHOOLCRAFT SHERMAN was held at the American church in Berlin on the afternoon of November 2, 1912, at 2 o'clock, the same hour as the funeral services in Utica.  The Berlin services were attended by the respective staffs of the American Embassy and the consulate general, headed by the ambassador, the Hon  John G A. Leishman, at whose suggestion the memorial was held   The German minister of foreign affairs sent Count Montgelas, of the foreign office, to attend the services as his representative.  Members of the American colony in Berlin also attended.

# TRIBUTES

BY PRESIDENT TAFT.

[From the Washington (D. C ) Post.]

NEW YORK, *October 30, 1912.*—President Taft was informed of the death of Vice President SHERMAN at 9.50 o'clock, as the Chief Executive and his Secretary of the Navy were seated in the Thirteenth Regiment Armory, Brooklyn, as guests of honor at a dinner given to them by employees of the Brooklyn Navy Yard, in celebration of the successful launching of the battleship *New York* to-day.

The President had just finished a plea for a greater Navy, and Commander Greaves of the navy yard was speaking at the time when the news of Mr SHERMAN's death was broken to the President.

Mr Taft at first made no comment after hearing the news. He remained seated, concealing emotions which he might have had, until Commander Greaves and Congressman Calder had finished their speeches. He then rose and said·

"MY FRIENDS· Three years ago you met on an occasion like this to celebrate the launching of the *Florida,* and you were honored by the presence of the Vice President of the United States—Vice President SHERMAN  It is a very sad duty for me to announce that word has just come that the Vice President is dead

"Those who knew him loved him  Those who knew the services he rendered to his country respected him.  I venture to ask that this assemblage adjourn in honor of his memory and that no further proceedings be taken "

A period of silence followed the President's unexpected words. The band came to the relief of the situation by playing, "My Country, 'Tis of Thee," and the naval officers and men filed out quickly.

The President was escorted to his automobile  Tears came to his eyes. He was lost sight of, however, as he stepped inside of the car and was whisked across Brooklyn Bridge and to the Pennsylvania Railroad Station in New York, where he was due to take his train at 12.30 o'clock for Washington.

Immediately after arriving in New York President Taft dispatched the following telegram to Mrs. Sherman at Utica

"Mrs. Taft and I extend to you our heartfelt sympathy in your great sorrow.  Our hearts go out to you in the loss of your noble and loving husband. Vice President SHERMAN had rendered distinguished service to his country, and his death, 10 years before the time allotted by the Psalmist, is a great loss. As a Member of Congress and a Vice President he endeared himself to all who knew him. His memory is full of sweetness and light.

"WILLIAM H TAFT."

Just before boarding his train for Washington President Taft made the following statement

"News of the death of Vice President JAMES S. SHERMAN has just reached me, and although it was not unexpected, it has filled my heart with sadness. I feel a sense of personal bereavement in the loss of a friend, who was a conscientious worker in the many undertakings in which we were engaged.

"It is an easy matter to pay tribute to his worth. He was a gentleman of splendid poise, of mental attainment, which were balanced by so fine a sense of justice that all who knew him respected him and admired him. The sobriquet which he has properly earned, and which was a tribute to a disposition that radiated sunshine and good will, readily explains the warm affection in which he was held by the many thousands who had come into personal contact with him

"As a legislator and expounder of parliamentary law and practice he had achieved a reputation of national proportions before he was elevated to the high and dignified office of Vice President of the United States His services as Vice President will be fittingly acknowledged by the United States Senate, over which he presided with marked fairness He was a Republican of sturdy principles, and his counsel within the party, always eagerly sought and highly regarded, will be sadly missed in the many crises created by new problems arising and demanding wise consideration and practical solution "

BY GOV WILSON.

[From the Utica (N Y) Daily Press, Nov 1, 1912.]

The family of Mr SHERMAN yesterday received hundreds of telegrams from all parts of the country expressing sympathy. Among them was the following:

"In common with the whole country, Mrs. Wilson and I have been deeply shocked by the death of Vice President SHERMAN, and we wish to extend to you our heartfelt sympathy.

"WOODROW WILSON."

[From the Utica (N. Y.) Daily Press, Nov 4, 1912 ]

ROCHESTER, *November 2, 1912.*—At the request of Gov. Wilson, the Democratic parade announced for this afternoon in New York City has been called off out of respect to the memory of Vice President SHERMAN, whose funeral will take place to-day.

[107]

As soon as Gov Woodrow Wilson arrived in Rochester late yesterday afternoon he telegraphed National Chairman W. F. McCombs to cancel the parade scheduled to be held in New York to-day by the College Men's Wilson and Marshall Clubs  The parade was to take place at the same hour that Vice President SHERMAN's funeral is to be held

The governor wired as follows:

"I hope that the arrangements for the parade will be canceled as an evidence of our deep sympathy for the family and friends of the late Vice President  I know this will be your feeling."

BY GOV. MARSHALL

[From the Washington (D C ), Post, Nov 1, 1912 ]

CHICAGO, *October 31, 1912.*—Gov. Thomas R Marshall, at the end of his 7,000-mile speaking tour to the Pacific Coast States and return, to-day canceled further campaign speeches because of the death of Vice President SHERMAN.  Gov. Marshall had been scheduled to make three speeches in Chicago and several in Indiana and Ohio

"In the presence of the dead," said Gov. Marshall, "every self-respecting man stands silent.

"Mr. SHERMAN is not alone the dead of one of the contesting political parties, but is the Nation's dead as well, and as such is deserving of the honor and respect of every man who respects the Nation "

Before departing from Chicago for Indianapolis this afternoon, Gov. Marshall sent a telegram of sympathy to Mrs. Sherman

BY COL ROOSEVELT

NEW YORK, *October 30, 1912.*—Just after he left the Madison Square Garden meeting, Col Roosevelt was informed of the death of Vice President SHERMAN.  The colonel immediately sent the following telegram

"Mrs. JAMES S SHERMAN, *Utica, N. Y* ·

"Mrs. Roosevelt and I are greatly shocked and concerned at the sad news of your husband's death.  We beg you to accept our most sincere sympathy.

"THEODORE ROOSEVELT "

NEW YORK, *November 1, 1912.*—The following telegram was sent by Chairman Prendergast, of the Progressive mass meeting in Madison Square Garden to-night, to Mrs. Sherman in response to Col Roosevelt's suggestion to the meeting

"Mrs. JAMES SCHOOLCRAFT SHERMAN, *Utica, N. Y.*

"At the suggestion of Theodore Roosevelt and in the name of 15,000 citizens of this city gathered in mass meeting, I have the

[108]

honor to extend to you their heartfelt sympathy in your great
sorrow.

"WILLIAM A. PRENDERGAST,
"Chairman."

OTHER EXPRESSIONS OF SYMPATHY

[From the Utica (N. Y.) Daily Press]

The universal esteem in which Mr. SHERMAN was held is testi-
fied to in the following messages of respect and sympathy to Mrs.
Sherman.

The following was received from Hon. Augustus O Bacon,
President pro tempore of the United States Senate·

"SHERRILL SHERMAN: As President pro tempore of the Senate I
have directed the Sergeant at Arms of the Senate to make all arrangements and provide everything which may be desired by your
family in connection with the funeral of your honored father, the
late Vice President, all of which it is desired may be entirely at
the charge of the Senate. So soon as you inform me of the arrangement and the dates fixed and desired by the family I will
cause the notices to be given to the Members of the Senate to secure their personal attendance. I beg that you will give me here
this information so soon as it may be found convenient to do so.

Senator Bacon also telegraphed as follows

"I beg to express my profound sympathy in this hour of your
unspeakable affliction in the death of your universally beloved
husband  By all the people of the United States his passing away
will be deplored as a great national loss, and by each Senator he
will be mourned as a personal friend"

"You have our heartfelt sympathy in your great sorrow. May
God bless you and yours.

"CHAMP CLARK,
"Speaker of the House of Representatives"

"All the members of the court deeply sympathize with you in
your great sorrow, and personally in the loss of so faithful a public servant.

"E D WHITE,
"Chief Justice, United States Supreme Court."

"Mrs. Hughes and I extend to you our deepest sympathy in
your great sorrow.

"CHARLES E. HUGHES."

"Mrs. Dix and I extend to you and your family our sympathy.
The State and the Nation have lost an honored and honorable
citizen.

"JOHN A. DIX,
"Governor of New York."

[109]

"I extend to you heart sympathy for the loss of your beloved husband, who was also my cherished friend
"CARDINAL GIBBONS."

"Mrs. Sulzer and myself are greatly shocked by the death of your distinguished husband, and in the hour of your sad bereavement we send you our heartfelt sympathy
"WILLIAM SULZER"

"Mrs. Straus and I deeply sympathize with you in your bereavement and grief. His cheerfulness and kindliness endeared your husband to all who knew him.
"OSCAR S STRAUS."

"Please accept my sympathy in your bereavement, and rest assured that your loss has brought sorrow to many. Your husband's friends are your friends.
"JOB E. HEDGES."

"The University of Notre Dame, Ind., mourns and prays beside you. May God comfort you and protect the Nation.
"PRESIDENT CAVANAUGH"

"WASHINGTON, D C
"Mrs Bryce and I and all the members of this embassy desire to convey our deep and sincere condolence with you in your great bereavement.
"BRITISH AMBASSADOR"

"WASHINGTON, D. C.
"At the request of the Japanese minister for foreign affairs and Viscountess Uchida, I beg to convey to you expression of their profound and sincerest condolence at the terrible bereavement of yourself and your family.
"VISCOUNT CHINDA,
"Japanese Ambassador"

"PLEASANTON, CAL
"May my wife and I offer you sincere sympathy in your great sorrow. Regret absence from the East will prevent my representing the Persian legation at the funeral.
"MIZRA ALI KULI KHAN,
"Persian Chargé d'Affaires"

"On behalf of the Swiss Government and the Nation I have the honor to express to you my profound sympathy.
"HENRI MARTIN,
"Chargé d'Affaires of Switzerland."

"TOKYO, JAPAN.
"My most sincere condolence and heartfelt sympathy
"PRINCE TOKUGAWA."

"Mrs Knox joins me in affectionate sympathy in your great bereavement.
"P. C. KNOX."

"My heartfelt sympathy goes out to you in this hour of grief. None will miss his kindly personality more than those who have known him so intimately during years of service in the Senate and House of Representatives.
"JOSEPH M DIXON."

"I grieve over the loss of one of my oldest and most valued friends Mrs Depew and I join in deepest and tenderest sympathy for yourself and family.
"CHAUNCEY M. DEPEW."

"I mourn with you and your family on the death of your distinguished husband and my friend, the Vice President. The Nation has lost an honest, wise, and courageous public servant, and to many there will come a deep sense of personal loss. Please accept the assurances of my sincere sympathy.
"J. G. CANNON."

Congressman William B. McKinley, of Illinois, who managed the preconvention Taft-Sherman campaign, said. "A great man and a good man has gone."

"SEATTLE, WASH.
"Our deepest sympathy in your great bereavement. The Nation has sustained a great loss in Mr SHERMAN's death
"W. E. HUMPHREY"

"SHREVEPORT, LA.
"In the death of your distinguished husband the Nation has lost one of its foremost citizens and faithful public servants. I served years in the House with Mr. SHERMAN. He enjoyed the esteem, confidence, and respect of his colleagues without regard to party. Mrs. Pujo joins me in extending heartfelt sympathy
"A. P. PUJO"

"Please accept my sympathy. The Nation and the State as well as the family have suffered a great loss.
"ALTON B. PARKER."

"Mrs. Odell and I sympathize with you in your bereavement. Many years of association with your husband gave me the right to call him friend, and his death therefore comes home to me with peculiar force. In his civic life he has ever been faithful, in every other walk of life he has been equally true  This knowledge should be of comfort to you in your hour of sorrow.

"B B. ODELL, Jr."

"WASHINGTON, D. C.
"Will you allow me to convey to you my personal sympathy and the sympathy of the Daughters of the American Revolution in the crushing sorrow which has come to you in the death of your distinguished husband.  The flag on our Memorial Continental Hall floats at half-mast in token of our respect and honor for the great man whose loss the Nation mourns.

"MRS. MATTHEW T. SCOTT,
"*President General, N. S. D. A. R.*"

"LUGANO, SWITZERLAND.
"We weep with you and yours

"LOUIS LOMBARD AND FAMILY."

"NEW YORK CITY.
"Please accept the deepest sympathy of my wife and myself in your great bereavement.

"JOHN PHILIP SOUSA."

"LONDON.
"I have lost a friend.  Deepest regret.

"HARRY LAUDER."

"SOUTH HARPSWELL, ME.
"Our deepest, sincerest, and lasting sympathy to you and yours in your irreparable affliction  We shall always be proud that we numbered in among his friends.

"REAR ADMIRAL AND MRS. PEARY."

"The Royal Arcanum of Illinois, in general meeting assembled in Chicago, in common with our fellow cousins throughout the United States, mourn the loss of our faithful brother, JAMES S SHERMAN, and tenders to you and to his sons, our bereaved brothers, our profound sympathy  He has served both his country and this order ably and nobly

"GEORGE W. MANIERRE,
"*Chairman.*
"F  T  McFADEN,
"*Supreme Regent.*
"GRAEME SMITH,
"*Grand Regent.*"

"MY DEAR MADAM· The members of Utica Lodge of Elks sympathize deeply with you in the loss of your husband  Mr SHERMAN

[112]

had been an Elk for over a score of years, a period in which he always showed an interest in our organization. We have lost an honored brother and our sorrow is deep at this time. Every one of the 700 Elks in Utica sends you heartfelt sympathy.

"LAWRENCE J. ZOBEL,
"Exalted Ruler."

"The members of Branch 51 of the Association of Letter Carriers of Fall River, Mass, extend to you their heartfelt sympathy in your sad bereavement. In your husband's death the Nation loses a faithful servant and the letter carriers a staunch friend.

"JOHN H. HAYTHORNTHWAITE,
"President"

"The Union League of Philadelphia sympathizes deeply with you and your family in this, your great sorrow. The Vice President was well known and greatly beloved here.

"WILLIAM T. TILDEN,
"President of the Union League."

Mrs. Jennie T. Hobart, widow of former Vice President Hobart, extended her sympathy as that of one "who can fully appreciate your great bereavement"

Former Vice President and Mrs. Fairbanks wired: "We loved him as a friend and loved him as an able and truthful public servant."

There also were expressions of profound sympathy from all the Cabinet ministers and from many American ministers to foreign countries as well as from foreign representatives in the United States. Whitelaw Reid spoke of the Vice President's death as "a great loss."

Messages of condolence were also received by Mrs. Sherman from the following. Senators George T. Oliver, J. H. Gallinger, Newell Sanders, A O Bacon, Luke Lea, Jeff Davis, C. A. Culberson, T. E. Burton, D. U. Fletcher, G. P. Wetmore, Isaac Stephenson, J W. Bailey, C. W. Watson, Charles E Townsend, W. E Chilton, John W. Kern, Charles Curtis, George ·Sutherland, W. A. Richardson, G. M. Hitchcock, W. Murray Crane, Boies Penrose, C. A. Swanson, Isidor Rayner, Thomas S. Martin, S. M. Cullom, Henry F Lippitt, George E. Chamberlain, Jonathan Bourne, jr., F. M Simmons, Henry F. Ashurst, Albert B Cummins, Robert J. Gamble, and James A. O'Gorman.

Also from the following Hon. Charles G Bennett, Secretary of the United States Senate, Hon. Frank S. Black, Attorney General George W. Wickersham, Rev. and Mrs. U. G. B. Pierce, Norman J. Gould, Hon. Dennis T. Flynn, Hon. Francis E. Hendricks, Hon.

Samuel McMillan, Hon. Eugene Hale, Hon. I. F. Fischer, Mr. and Mrs George Sicard, Secretary of War Henry L. Stimson, Brother Gregory, Henry Casson, jr., Hon. Jacob Ruppert, jr., Hon. W. B. McKinley, Walter C. Witherbee, Señor Don Juan Riaño, ambassador of Spain, and Madame De Riaño; George Therrill, Mr. and Mrs E. H. Wells, W C Hackett, Hon. James R. Garfield, Hon Frank H. Hiscock, Judge Irving G Vann, Hon. George B. McClellan, J. G. Schmidtlapp, J D Fuller, B. S Rodey, Judge Warren B. Hooker, Louis Fisher, Mr. and Mrs. Philip Elting, Hon. Carmi A. Thompson, secretary to the President, Samuel P. Calef, George C. Priestley, P B Boden, Hon. Richard Bartholdt, Mrs. Ethel McCarey Sanger, Hon Charles L Knapp, Mr. and Mrs. Pensel, Mr. and Mrs. Louis J. Ehret, J. C. P. Kincaid, F. W Buderus, Charles A. Hawley, F S. Hill, Mr. and Mrs. William Roach, John W. Van Allen, Robert Gardiner McGregor, D. M. Johnson, J. Frank Aldrich, Hon. John T. Mott, John C. Moffitt, J. C. Eversman, A V. Conover, Garry B Adams, H M. Daugherty, H W. Dearborn, Mr. and Mrs. William Morris, Hon. John Dalzell, J J Gilbert, N B. Yates, John E. Dowd, Col William M Griffith, William R. P. Bloyer, Martin J. Hutchins, R. A. C. Smith, M. D. Crowley, C. W. Richardson, Ormsby McCammon, Hon. C. L. Bartlett, W. C. Warren, William Clift Foote, I. P. Brown, Charles E. Fitch, Victor Rosewater, Wilfrid Hartley, Reuben R Lyon, Hon. Charles R. Skinner, M W. Blumenburg, George W. Wanamaker, Hon. Charles A. Towne, George C. Boldt, George X. McLenahan, Mr. and Mrs. V. M. Wilson, jr., James Otis Woodward, J. G. Searne, H. H. Knowles, F B. Newell, Mr. and Mrs Arthur W. Sewall, Mr and Mrs Homer P. Snyder, Hon Henry M Goldfogle, Hon D. F Lafean, Hon. J Van Vechten Olcott, Mrs. Kate I Nixon, S G. Malby, Gonsalo De Quesada, Hon. Charles H Sherrill, Col D M Ransdell, Sergeant at Arms United States Senate; B. N. Martin, Marcus P. Rice, William A. Logue, Mr. and Mrs E A. Brooks, the German Ambassador and Countess Bernstorff, Hon George W Aldridge, Hon. William Barnes, jr., Hon George S. Klock, Miss May Irwin, the French Ambassador and Mme. Jusserand, George Orvis, A E Martin, Mr. and Mrs William H. Watson, Fred A. Smith, Thomas E. Oshen, Mr. and Mrs. John W. Vrooman, Henry M. Rose, C. B. McCawley, Hon. George Puchta, Hon. and Mrs. Charles Dick, Mrs Elizabeth H. Hemphill, James K Apgar, Bessie Edwards, Mr. and Mrs David M. Ranken, Hon and Mrs Richard Wayne Parker, Mr. and Mrs A Seeley, Francis A. Willard, Howard B. French, George E. Hopkins, J. E. Millholland, Mrs. A. S. Paddock, Hon. W. B Greene, Gen. W. W. Wotherspoon, Louis V. Davison, David F. Wilder, Ralph A. Gamble, Justice of the Supreme Court Joseph McKenna, Lloyd Paul Stryker, Hon. Nicholas Murray Butler, Hon. Montague Lessler, Hon. C. H. Duell, A. B. Andrews, Dr. M. O. Terry, S. C. Neale, Mr. and Mrs. Robert Burch, E. J. Welsh, Hon. L. P. Fuhrmann, mayor of Buffalo, Mr. and Mrs. E. F. Murray, Mr. and Mrs. William H. Hotchkiss, Mr. and Mrs. Charles B. Brooker, John

C. Williams, Mr. and Mrs. Frederick H Elliott, Frederick S. Flower, the Danish minister, Mr. and Mrs. Charles Henry Butler, Hon William Richardson, Charles F. Newsom, Mrs. George M. Pullman, Mayor Scanlon, Lawrence, Mass; Sterling J Joiner, Mrs. Mary Townsend, Hon Horace White, C L. Stone, J Herbert Ballantine, George H Harris, Secretary of the Treasury Franklin MacVeagh, the Japanese Ambassador Viscount Chinda, Mr. and Mrs. P. W. Herrick, Mr. and Mrs. Carl Stone, H. B. Tompkins, Mr. and Miss Hawk, Hon. Samuel Koenig, the Minister of Norway and Mme. Bryn, Hon and Mrs Truman H. Newberry, Mrs. Caroline Caton Williams and daughter, H. P. Bells, the senior class, Berkeley Institute, Brooklyn, N. Y.; Hon and Mrs. Timothy L Woodruff, the Haitian minister, United States Supreme Court Justice Mahlon Pitney, Hon. and Mrs. James R. Mann, Mr. and Mrs. L. White Busbey, Mr. and Mrs. William C Denny, the governor of New Hampshire, Robert P. Bass; Hon L B Gleason, Mr and Mrs. Ellsworth Brown, Cortland S Wheeler, Mr. and Mrs. L. A. Coolidge, Mr. and Mrs James M E. O'Grady, Hon. and Mrs. Charles B Law, John L. E. Pell, Louis Waldauer, Hon. and Mrs. J. Charles Linthicum, Mr George C. Van Tuyl, jr, Mr. George Hinman, Mr. Jules Roth, Mr. Harry S Jackson, Mr. and Mrs. Seth C. Adams, Mr. and Mrs. F. W. Sessions, Thora Reynolds, Miss Mabel T. Boardman, Mr. and Mrs. William C. Sylvester, Hon John Barrett, Mr. and Mrs John Hays Hammond, Postmaster General Frank A. Hitchcock, the Chargé d'Affaires of the Republic of Panama and Mrs. Brin, Epsilon Chapter of Sigma Phi, Ithaca, N. Y., Hon. J. Hampton Moore, The Ohio Society of the City of New York, Mr. and Mrs. Frank S. Witherbee, Mr and Mrs Benjamin S Minor, R. F. Brush, J. F. McMurray, Mr. and Mrs. William Littauer, Irving W. Day, John F. Fitzgerald, mayor of Boston, Hon. Newton W. Gilbert, Martin J Bowe, J. A Flannigan, Hon. Joseph B Foraker, Paul S. Pearsall, Mrs. Charles J. Hughes, jr., Miss Christine Hoar, Hon and Mrs. J W. Fordney, Mrs. W. B Newman, N. Main, Commander and Viscountess Benoist d'Azy, United States Supreme Court Justice and Mrs. Lurton, Leroy W. Baldwin, S. C. Neale, Maj. Richard Sylvester, Señor Antonio Martin Rivero, Cuban minister; Mr. and Mrs Frederick C. Stevens, the Board of Bishops of the M. E. Church of Toledo, Ohio, Evangeline Booth, John E Frost, F. R Bane, George E. Vankennen, Francis E. Ames, Hon. Nicholas and Alice Longworth, Hon. J. Sloat Fassett, Mr. and Mrs. W R Wilcox, Royal Arcanum of the State of Ohio, H D Oliver, Gen. Oscar F. Long, Rev. Father Wilham H. Ketcham, Mr. and Mrs Edson Bradley, Isabella E. Mullholland, G. Gunby Jordan, Philip A Howard, Florence M Bennett, C K. Corbin, Wilbur E. Van Auken, Curtice Brothers, Hon. L W. Emerson, Walter M. Ostrander, J Shepard, jr., Mr and Mrs. George C. Wood, Raymond F. Rode, Mr and Mrs. F. H. Judd, Mr. and Mrs. Frederick Smith, Hon. T. Harvey Ferris, Hon. James K O'Connor, Hon. Charles D. Walcott, J. J. Guernsey, Taft Business Men's League of St. Paul, Minn., Hon. and Mrs. W. A.

Massey, Mrs William B Heyburn, R. L Kers, jr, W. R. Roach, Miles P. Ondereaux, Hon. and Mrs. W. S Cowbridge, the Minister of The Netherlands and Mme. Loudon, Charles H. Wilson, Rev. John Arthur, William R. P. Bloyer, Ellis A. Gimel, Hon. James K. McGuire, Henry White Callahan, Cary F. Simmons, Mr. and Mrs. William A. Shanklin, Hon. Herbert Parsons, Hon. George B. Cortelyou, P. A. Franklin, Charles G. Wagner, Sophonisba P. Breckenridge, Hon. and Mrs. Frederick M Davenport, Fay T. Kent, Herbert W Clark, E. C. Converse, Commander Joseph W. Kay, Hon G. Fred Talbott, G. W. Graham, Mayor John J. Irving, Binghamton; Mrs. Percy Morgan, Hon. John W. Weeks, Hon. William L. Ward, Pittsburgh Association of Credit Men; Supreme Court Justice Willis Van Devanter, the Bolivian minister and family, George Alexander, mayor of Los Angeles, George T. Stockham, Hon. James McKinney, Hon Daniel A. Driscoll, J. S. Runnells, Henry H. Bender, Mathilda Gerry, Hon. Edward Bruce Moore, Mrs. George R. Malby, A. Garrison McClintock, Hon. Charles W. Fairbanks, Royal Arcanum of Oregon, Judge Peter B McLennan, Hon J M. Levy, Hon. John Stewart, Hon. Nelson W. Aldrich, James M Belden, Hon. George von L. Meyer, Secretary of the Navy, Hon. Charles Burke, Hon. E. F. Kinkead, F. H. Murphy, William B. Austin, for Hamilton Club, Chicago; Andrew J. Lester, for Chicago Club, Mme. Bakhméteff, wife of the ambassador of Russia, Miss Mary Schluter, Miss Sally H. Culberson, S V. Whelen, Chief Justice White, for the justices of the United States Supreme Court; Chief Justice and Mrs. Edward D. White, Hon Charles F. Scott, Hon. William Lorimer, the Chinese minister, Chang Yin Tang, Greek Chargé d'Affaires Caftanzoglu, Mr. and Mrs. A. J. Harty, Margaret M Rager, Frank E. Wilson, the Peruvian minister, F A. Pezet; Mr. and Mrs Caldwell Sweet, William Busby, Carl Harrer, Hon. and Mrs. Julius Kahn, Hon and Mrs S. W. McCall, Irving C Casler, M. J. Sherrill, Hon. Alton B. Parker, Hon. and Mrs. George S Legare, Ida H. Crany, Mr. and Mrs. Arthur Ramsey, for the students and faculty of Fairmont Seminary, Washington, D. C., H. M. Baker, for the Chevy Chase Seminary, Washington, D. C; the Turkish ambassador, Youssouf Zia Pacha; Mrs William E Curtis, C. K. MacDougall, Stewart Lowery, Hon I W. Wood, Hon. and Mrs W. W. Cocks, Anna Ray Root, Edith Patten Corbin, Hon. Thomas W Bradley, and Arnold Shanklin, United States consul general, City of Mexico

# CONDOLENCES FROM FOREIGN GOVERNMENTS

## ARABIA

From Maj H. F. Jacob, first assistant political resident of Aden, Arabia, to the American consul at Aden, November 6, 1912.

"I have the honor to acknowledge the receipt of your letter of the 2d November, 1912, and to convey to you the expression of the political resident's deepest regret at the news of the sad death of His Excellency JAMES SCHOOLCRAFT SHERMAN, the Vice President of the United States."

## ARGENTINA

From President Roque Saenz Pena, of Argentina, to President Taft:

"BUENOS AIRES, *October 31, 1912*—Pray accept, Excellency, the expressions of my condolence for the regrettable death of the eminent citizen Mr. JAMES SHERMAN, Vice President of the Republic."—(Cablegram, translation.)

From Mr. Manuel E. Malbrán, chargé d'affaires of the Argentine Republic, Washington, to the Secretary of State, October 31, 1912·

"I have the honor to acknowledge the receipt of this day's communication by which the Secretary of State is pleased to announce the sad intelligence of the death of the Hon. JAMES S. SHERMAN, Vice President of the United States of America.

"In offering to the department, in the name of my Government and in my own, the most heartfelt expressions of condolence on the mourning which means so great a loss to the Nation, I make it my duty to inform you that appropriate measures have been taken at the legation to keep the Argentine flag at half-mast on the building as long as the official mourning lasts"

Department of State, November 1, 1912, memorandum·

"The chargé d'affaires of the Argentine Republic called to say he had received a telegram from his Government directing him to present the sincere condolences of Argentina on the death of the Vice President. He will address a note to the department. Mr. Adee told the chargé d'affaires that a copy would be sent to Mrs. Sherman."

From Mr Manuel E. Malbrán to the Secretary of State, November 1, 1912:

"In compliance with express instructions from my Government, forwarded by cable to the legation, I have the honor to present to the Government of the United States the expressions of the Argentine Government's condolence on the lamented death of the Vice President of the Nation, the Hon. JAMES S. SHERMAN.

"The high attainments and great moral gifts of the Hon. JAMES S. SHERMAN were well known and highly appreciated in the Argentine Republic and my Government desires to express to that of the United States the sincereness of the sentiments with which it joins in the mourning of this Nation for the loss of one of its most notable personalities.

"In begging the Secretary of State kindly to convey to the Most Excellent the President of the United States the Argentine Government's expressions of condolence, to which I join my own, I have pleasure in renewing to the Secretary of State the assurance of my highest and most distinguished consideration."

### AUSTRIA-HUNGARY

From Baron Erich Zwiedinek von Sudenhorst, chargé d'affaires of Austria-Hungary, Washington, to the Secretary of State, November 2, 1912:

"I have had the honor to receive your excellency's communication of October 31 last, relative to the death of Mr. JAMES SCHOOLCRAFT SHERMAN, Vice President of the United States.

"I have received instructions from the Imperial and Royal Government to express its genuine sympathy to the Government of the United States on the occasion of this deplorable loss.

"Taking the liberty of having recourse to your excellency's good offices in carrying out my instructions, I beg your excellency also to accept the expression of my own sincere sympathy."

### BELGIUM

Department of State, November 1, 1912, memorandum:

"The Belgian minister called upon Mr. Adee to-day to say he had a telegram from his Government directing him to express sincere condolence on the loss of the Vice President"

From Mr. E Havenith, Belgian minister, Washington, to the Secretary of State, November 1, 1912:

"With profound regret did I hear the sad intelligence of the death of the Hon. JAMES SCHOOLCRAFT SHERMAN, Vice President of the United States.

"I have the honor to beg you to accept my sincere condolence on the occasion of the death of that statesman in whose death the country suffered so trying a loss.

"I have been instructed by my Government to convey to the Government of the United States the expression of its deep condolence."

### BOLIVIA

From Señor Don I. Calderon, Bolivian minister, Washington, to the Secretary of State, November 1, 1912:

"I have heard with true sorrow of the death of the Vice President of the United States, the Hon. JAMES SCHOOLCRAFT SHERMAN, which took place at Utica on October 30 last.

"I beg your excellency to accept my Government's and my own heartfelt expression of sympathy in the loss of the distinguished citizen who so creditably discharged his high duties."

### BRAZIL

From Mr. D. da Gama, Brazilian ambassador, Washington, to the Secretary of State, October 31, 1912

"In the name of my President I have the honor to apply to your excellency with a request that you be pleased to convey to the President of the Republic the expression of sincere condolence on the part of the Government and people of Brazil on the national mourning brought upon the United States of America by the lamented death of Vice President SHERMAN. To these expressions I beg leave to add my own personal regrets to your excellency, to whom I have the honor to renew the assurances of my highest consideration.

### CHILE

From President Ramon Barros Luco of Chile to President Taft.

"SANTIAGO, *November 2, 1912.*—My Government and the Chilean people profoundly deplore the bereavement which afflicts the great American Nation in the death of its illustrious Vice President SHERMAN."—(Cablegram, translation )

Department of State, October 31, 1912, memorandum.

"The Chilean minister called to-day upon Mr Adee to express to him his sincere regret at the death of the Vice President; and to express sorrow on behalf of the Chilean Government."

From Señor Don Edo. Suarez Mejia, Chilean minister, Washington, D. C., to the Secretary of State, November 1, 1912.

"I have the honor to receive your excellency's obliging note of yesterday's date, intended to confirm to me the sorrowful news of the death at Utica, at 9.42 p m last evening, of the most excellent Mr. JAMES SCHOOLCRAFT SHERMAN, Vice President of the United States.

"In discharge of a painful duty, I offer to your excellency in the name of the Government of Chile the expression of its deep condolence on the taking off of the illustrious citizen who, by popular verdict and with the respect of the whole country, held the high office of Vice President of the Republic.

"For my part I wish to confirm the sentiments I had the honor personally to express to your excellency yesterday most sincerely showing the sorrow which afflicts the Government and people of the United States"

### CHINA

From Mr Chang Yin Tang, Chinese minister, Washington, to the Secretary of State, November 1, 1912

"I have the honor to acknowledge the receipt of your note of the 31st ultimo, announcing the death at Utica, N. Y., at 9.42 o'clock p. m., on Wednesday, October 30, 1912, of the Hon JAMES SCHOOLCRAFT SHERMAN, Vice President of the United States.

"I have cabled to my Government this sad intelligence, and I beg to offer to the Government and people of the United States the heartfelt sympathy of the Government and people of China in the loss of a great statesman whose nobility of character won the love and respect of all."

From Mr. Chang Yin Tang to the Secretary of State, November 2, 1912:

"I have the honor to inform you that I have just received a cable message addressed to the President of the United States by the President of the Republic of China, of which the following is an English translation.

"'Mr PRESIDENT: I learn with inexpressible grief of the death of the Vice President of the United States   The people of China join with me in mourning for the distinguished statesman.  I beg to extend to you my personal sympathy and the sympathy of the people of China.

> "'YUAN SHI-KAI,
> "'*President of China.*'

"I have the honor to request that you will be so kind as to convey the above message to its high destination."

### COLOMBIA

From Señor Don Julio Betancourt, minister of Colombia, Washington, to the Secretary of State, November 1, 1912:

"I have received the very obliging communication by which you announced to me the lamented death of the Hon. JAMES SCHOOLCRAFT SHERMAN, Vice President of the United States.

"In the name of my Government and in my own I extend, through you, to the Government and people of the United States the expression of the most profound regret at the taking off of so distinguished a citizen.

"As a sign of mourning for this national loss, the flag of Colombia has been displayed at half-mast at the office of the legation."

From Señor Don Pedro M. Carreño, minister for foreign affairs of Colombia, to the American chargé d'affaires at Bogota, November 4, 1912:

"By your courteous note, F. O. No. 42, of yesterday's date, this office has been informed to its sincere sorrow of the death of His Excellency JAMES SHERMAN, Vice President of the United States, which occurred on October 30 last. The national flag will therefore remain at half-mast until to-day."

### COSTA RICA

Department of State, October 31, 1913, memorandum.

"The minister of Costa Rica called upon Mr. Adee to-day to express on behalf of his Government and of himself, personally, sorrow for the death of Vice President SHERMAN. He will send an informal note to the department to this effect."

From Señor Don Joaquin Bernardo Calvo, minister of Costa Rica, Washington, to the Secretary of State, October 31, 1912:

"Referring to my visit of to-day, and interpreting the sentiments of my Government, I have the honor to confirm my expressions of deep sorrow for the lamentable death of the Hon. JAMES S SHERMAN, Vice President of the United States, and, at the same time, I beg leave to request of you very kindly to transmit to Mrs Sherman our heartfelt sentiments of condolence on her bereavement."

From Señor Don Joaquin Bernardo Calvo to the Secretary of State, November 1, 1912:

"With profound sorrow I have been notified by your note of yesterday that the Hon. JAMES SCHOOLCRAFT SHERMAN died at Utica, N. Y, and that the funeral will take place in that city to-morrow at 2 p. m.

"On this sad occasion, I have received from my Government instructions to express in its name to the Washington Government the most sincere condolence on the lamented loss of a citizen possessed of the high merits and conspicuous civic virtues by which the prominent functionary the Hon. Mr. SHERMAN was distinguished when alive.

"In so carrying out the wishes of my Government, I beg your leave, Mr. Secretary, to join to this manifestation of mourning my own expression of like sentiments of sorrow."

### CUBA

From Señor Lcdo. Antonio Martin-Rivero, Cuban minister, Washington, D. C., to the Secretary of State, October 31, 1912:

"In the name of the Government and people of Cuba, in my own, and in that of all the members of the legation, I have the honor to offer to you the assurances of my deep sympathy in the grief that is now weighing upon the American Nation by reason of the death of the Hon. JAMES S. SHERMAN, Vice President of the United States "

Department of State, November 1, 1912, memorandum:
" The Cuban minister called to express deep sympathy on the part of Cuba at the death of the Vice President   The minister will address a note to the department to this effect."

From Señor R. Gutierrez Alcaide, charge d'affaires of Cuba at Panama, to the American charge d'affaires, November 1, 1912:
" With deep sorrow I have just acquainted myself by reading the cable messages published to-day in the newspapers of this capital of the sudden death of the Hon. Mr. SHERMAN, Vice President of the United States of America, and in offering to you as the worthy representative of the noble American Nation the expression of my most heartfelt sympathy for such unfortunate news, I wish to assure you that I join heartily in the feeling of sorrow which to-day afflicts the American people and their brothers of all America."

### DENMARK

From Mr. C Brun, Danish minister, Washington, to the Secretary of State, October 31, 1912:
" In the name of my Government which I have the honor to represent, and in my own, I beg to express to you, and through you to the Government of the United States, my most sincere and deep-felt sorrow and sympathy in the great loss which the American Nation has suffered by the death yesterday of the Vice President of the United States, JAMES SCHOOLCRAFT SHERMAN."

### DOMINICAN REPUBLIC

From Señor Dr Don Francisco J. Peynado, Dominican minister, Washington, to the Secretary of State, November 1, 1912:
" With the most profound sorrow have I received the sad news of the death of the Hon. JAMES SCHOOLCRAFT SHERMAN, Vice President of the United States, which occurred at Utica, N. Y., on Wednesday, the 30th of October, 1912, at 9.42 p. m.
" An illustrious citizen, eminent servant of his country, is thus removed from the scene, and in the presence of the irreparable loss, the Dominican people and Government join with the people and Government of the United States in sharing with them the fitting feelings of regret occasioned by his unlooked-for removal."

### ECUADOR

From President Plaza, of Ecuador, to President Taft:
" QUITO, ECUADOR, *November 5, 1912* —The Government and people of Ecuador lament the regrettable death of His Excellency

Vice President SHERMAN, and share the grief of Your Excellency and of the American people.—(Cablegram, translation.)

From Señor Dr. Don S. S. Wither S., chargé d'affaires of Ecuador, Washington, to the Secretary of State, October 31, 1912

"With profound sorrow my Government has learned of the death of the Vice President of the United States, Mr JAMES S. SHERMAN, and I have been specially directed by cable to present to you, in behalf of the Government and people of Ecuador, the heartiest manifestation of condolence for the irreparable loss that the American Nation has suffered.

"In complying with the wishes of my Government, I have the honor to avail myself of this opportunity to express to you the sincere expression of my personal sympathy."

### EGYPT

From Y. Wahba, ministry for foreign affairs, Cairo, to the American consul general, November 3, 1912:

"I have the honor to acknowledge receipt of your telegram of yesterday's date informing me of the death of Mr. J. S. SHERMAN, Vice President of the United States.

"The Government of His Highness the Khedive, deeply feeling as it does the mourning of the American Nation, charges me to beg you to be toward the Government of the Republic the interpreter of its most profound regret and sincere sympathy."

### FRANCE

From Mr J. J. Jusserand, French ambassador, Washington, to the Secretary of State, November 1, 1912

"I have received the letter by which your excellency did me the honor to impart to me the sad intelligence of the death of the Hon. JAMES SCHOOLCRAFT SHERMAN, Vice President of the United States.

"I am transmitting the information to my Government, which, your excellency may be assured, will take a sincere part in the mourning of the President of the United States and the American Nation.

"I beg leave to extend to you, Mr. Secretary of State, the expression of my personal condolence on so sad an event. I know it is for you the loss of a friend, and having had, for my part, many occasions to appreciate his high gifts, I can not but fully realize the sorrow you must undergo."

### GERMANY

Department of State, November 1, 1912, memorandum:

"The Imperial German ambassador called to express the condolence of his Government on the death of the Vice President, and

[123]

his own personal sympathy at the loss of a warm friend He will write a note to the department."

From Count J. H. von Bernstorff, German ambassador, Washington, to the Secretary of State, November 1, 1912:

"I have the honor to acknowledge the receipt of your excellency's note of the 31st of October last by which you gave me notice of the highly to be lamented death of the Vice President of the United States. I beg leave to express to the Government of the United States my most sincere sympathy in this severe and distressing loss. I shall never forget the friendly relations that I maintained with the deceased. I expect to have an opportunity to-day to express orally to your excellency my most deeply felt condolence."

### GREAT BRITAIN

From the Right Hon. James Bryce, British ambassador, Washington, to the Secretary of State, November 1, 1912.

"I have the honor to acknowledge receipt of your note of October 31 in which you convey to me the distressing news of the death of the Vice President of the United States.

"I desire to convey to you an expression of the sincere regret and sympathy of my Government, and also of my personal sorrow, at the loss suffered by the people of the United States. I have already personally conveyed my condolences to the President "

Department of State, November 4, 1912, memorandum:

"The British ambassador called upon the Acting Secretary of State to-day to say that he was instructed to formally convey the deep condolences of his Government upon the death of the Vice President. The ambassador spoke feelingly of his personal regret and sympathy. He had known Mr. SHERMAN well for many years, and regarded him as one of the ablest heads the Senate ever had He said he had a keen appreciation of the loss the entire country would sustain without Mr. SHERMAN's eminent services and kindly counsels.

"Mr. Adee thanked the ambassador for his words, and spoke of Mr. SHERMAN as having been especially a lover of peace and beloved of everyone."

### GREECE

Department of State, November 4, 1912, memorandum:

"Mr. Caftanzoglu, the chargé d'affaires of Greece, called to-day upon the Acting Secretary of State, Mr. Adee, to say that he had received a cable from his Government directing him to express sincere condolence on the part of the Greek Government at the death of the Vice President, and also to extend the personal sympathy of the minister for foreign affairs on the lamentable death of this great public man."

GUATEMALA

From President M. Estrada Cabrera, of Guatemala, to President Taft:

"GUATEMALA, *November 2, 1912.*—In the name of the people and Government of Guatemala I hasten to send to Your Excellency and the Government over which you preside the most sincere expression of condolence on the death of the Vice President, Mr. SHERMAN."—(Cablegram, translation.)

From Señor Luis Toledo Herrarte, minister for foreign affairs of Guatemala, to the Secretary of State:

"GUATEMALA.—I beg your excellency to deign to convey to the Government and people of the United States the expression of heartfelt condolence of the Guatemalan people and Government on the occasion of the lamented demise of the Hon. JAMES S. SHERMAN, Vice President of the United States."—(Cablegram, translation.)

From Señor Luis Toledo Herrarte, minister of foreign affairs of Guatemala, to American chargé d'affaires at Guatemala City, November 2, 1912:

"By the esteemed note of your honor, No. 270, of even date, I have heard with great sorrow of the death of the Hon. Vice President SHERMAN, which took place on the 30th of last October.

"In the name of the Government of the Republic, I comply with the duty of expressing to your honor the most heartfelt condolence for the irreparable loss which the people and the Government of the United States have suffered by his death."

From Señor Don Joaquin Mendez, Guatemalan minister, Washington, to the Acting Secretary of State, October 31, 1912:

"I have the honor to acknowledge with the deepest sorrow your esteemed note of this date informing me of the sorrowful tidings of the death of the Hon. JAMES SCHOOLCRAFT SHERMAN, Vice President of the United States.

"I wish to express to your excellency in the name of the Government of Guatemala and the people of my country the deepest sympathy on the occasion of the sad death of the honorable Vice President of the United States.

"The death of the honorable Vice President of the United States can not fail to bring sorrow into the hearts of all. But the memory of his noble deeds and heroic sacrifices will survive.

"I beg you to accept, your excellency, my own deepest personal sympathy for the lamentable bereavement of the honorable Vice President"

From Señor Don Joaquin Mendez to the Secretary of State, November 4, 1912:

"The profound sorrow and intense grief caused among the members of the Government and the people of Guatemala by the most lamented intelligence of the death of the Hon. Vice President SHERMAN have been reflected in two cablegrams that I have received, one from President M. Estrado Cabrera, the other from Minister Toledo Herrarte, both carrying the expression of the keenest sympathy and most sincere regret to the Government and people of the United States of America and most particularly to His Excellency the President of the United States and the most excellent the Secretary of State I therefore beg your excellency to deign to accept these expressions as a fresh evidence of the cordiality of our relations and of the community of interests which Guatemala always desires to maintain with her elder sister, the great American Republic. At the same time I shall thank your excellency if you will please to consider this note a continuation of that which I had the honor to address to you on October 31 last and accept the homage of my highest consideration and high esteem "

### HAITI

From Mr. Solon Menos, Haitian minister, Washington, to the Secretary of State, November 1, 1912:

" In acknowledging the receipt of your letter announcing the death of the Hon JAMES SCHOOLCRAFT SHERMAN, Vice President of the United States, I beg you to accept the sincere condolence I have it at heart to extend to you in the name of my Government and my own on the grievous loss your Government and country have sustained in the death of the illustrious decedent "

### HONDURAS

Department of State, October 31, 1912, memorandum:

" The minister of Honduras called upon Mr. Adee to-day to express the regret of his Government, and his personal regret, at the loss of Vice President SHERMAN. He will also send an informal note to the department to this effect."

From Dr Albert Membreño, minister of Honduras, Washington, to the Secretary of State, October 31, 1912:

" Deep was my sorrow on hearing of the death of the Hon. JAMES SCHOOLCRAFT SHERMAN, Vice President of the Republic. The demise of that great statesman, whose life may be taken as a model for its eminent virtues, is a loss to the American Nation and to the Latin countries which the deceased loved so well. I have apprized my Government of the sad event by cable; and faithfully voicing the sentiments of the Honduran people and yielding to my own, I heartily join in the sorrow that is now bowing the American people on account of the death of one of their most illustrious sons."

[126]

From Dr. Albert Membreño to the Secretary of State, November 1, 1912:

"I have had the honor to receive your excellency's obliging note of the 31st of October last by which you announce to me the death, at Utica, N. Y., at 9.42 p m., on Wednesday, October 30, 1912, of the Hon. JAMES SCHOOLCRAFT SHERMAN, Vice President of the United States, and that the funeral will take place in the same city of Utica on Saturday, November 2, at 2 p. m.

"The President of Honduras, to whom I cabled that very sad event, has just sent me a message directing me to express his most sincere condolence to the Most Excellent the President."

### ITALY

From Mr. Giuseppe Catalani, chargé d'affaires, Italian Embassy, Washington, to the Secretary of State, November 3, 1912·

"I have the honor to acknowledge the receipt of the note, dated October 31 last, by which I am advised of the death of the Hon. JAMES SCHOOLCRAFT SHERMAN, Vice President of the United States, which took place at Utica, N Y, at 9.42 p. m. Wednesday, October 30, 1912.

"In expressing to your excellency my keen sympathy in the untimely loss of that illustrious man, I have the honor to inform you that I have not failed to cable the mournful intelligence to my Government, which, I am sure, will share the sorrow and mourning of the President and this great Nation.

"I regret that my official duties prevented my attending, as I most earnestly desired to do, the funeral which took place at Utica on the 2d instant."

### JAPAN

From Viscount Sutemi Chinda, Japanese ambassador, Washington, to the Secretary of State, October 31, 1912.

"I have the honor to acknowledge the receipt of your communication informing me of the death of the Hon. JAMES SCHOOLCRAFT SHERMAN, Vice President of the United States, and I beg to tender you expression of my profound sympathy and condolence at the painful loss befallen the Government and people of the United States I have duly conveyed to my Government the sad intelligence communicated to me in your note under acknowledgment.

From Viscount Sutemi Chinda to the Secretary of State, November 1, 1912:

"Under telegraphic instructions just received from his Imperial Majesty's Government, I have the honor to convey to you, and through you to your Government, the assurance of the most sincere sentiments of grief and sorrow with which my Government shares in the loss sustained by the American Government and people through the deeply lamented death of the Hon. James Schoolcraft Sherman, Vice President of the United States."

### MEXICO

From President Francisco I. Madero, of Mexico, to President Taft:

"Mexico City, Mexico, *October 31, 1912.*—Will Your Excellency please accept the sincere condolence of the Mexican people and Government, and my own, on the death of Vice President Sherman "—(Telegram, translation.)

From the Hon. Pedro Lascurain, minister for foreign affairs of Mexico, to the Secretary of State, October 31, 1912:

"Will your excellency be pleased to convey to your Government the Mexican Government's heartfelt condolence on the death of Vice President Sherman."—(Telegram, translation.)

From Señor Don Arturo de la Cueva, the Mexican chargé d'affaires, Washington, to the Secretary of State, October 31, 1912:

"I have had the honor to receive your note of to-day by which your excellency informed me of the death of the Most Excellent Mr. James Schoolcraft Sherman, Vice President of the United States of America, at Utica, N. Y., on Wednesday, the 30th of October.

"In expressing to your excellency the most sincere sentiments of condolence of the embassy's staff on the distressing loss sustained by the Government and people of the United States, I renew to you the assurances of my highest and most distinguished consideration "

### NETHERLANDS

From Jonkheer J. Loudon, minister of The Netherlands, Washington, to the Secretary of State, November 1, 1912·

"I have had the honor to receive your excellency's letter of yesterday's date, by which you apprise me of the sorrowful loss just sustained by the United States in the death of Mr. James S. Sherman, Vice President of the Republic.

"Under the sad circumstances, I have the honor to have recourse to your excellency's habitual kindness and to ask that you may be pleased to acquaint the President of the United States with the share I take in this national mourning, and I beg leave also to offer to your excellency my most sincere condolences."

### NICARAGUA

From President Diaz, of Nicaragua, to President Taft·

"Managua, *November 2, 1912.*—Nicaraguan Government and people join in mourning of American Government and people for death Hon Vice President SHERMAN "—(Telegram, translation )

"MANAGUA, *November 3, 1912.*—Deign to accept the condolence of Nicaragua and my own sentiments of sympathy in the American national mourning for the grievous death of the Hon Vice President JAMES SHERMAN "—(Telegram, translation.)

From Diego Manuel Chamorro, minister for foreign affairs of Nicaragua, to the Secretary of State:

"MANAGUA, NICARAGUA, *November 2, 1912.*—Government deplores death Hon. Vice President SHERMAN, and for this grievous national loss offers its condolence to your excellency and your Government."

From Mr. Salvador Castrillo, minister of Nicaragua, Washington, to the Secretary of State, November 1, 1912:

"I acknowledge the receipt of your excellency's obliging and feeling note, dated yesterday, by which you deign to apprise me of the death at Utica, N. Y., on Wednesday, the 30th of October, at 9.42 p. m., of the Hon. JAMES SCHOOLCRAFT SHERMAN, Vice President of the United States, and you add that the funeral will take place at Utica, to-morrow, Saturday, November 2, at 2 p m.

"I have reported to my Government the sad event which brings mourning to the American Nation that loses in the Vice President not only a very high functionary, who did it honor, but also one of its most illustrious public men, in whom it can take pride.

"The Republic of Nicaragua and my Government join the American people and Government in lamenting his removal and take part in their mourning.

"I beg your excellency to deign to convey, when convenient, to the Most Excellent the President the assurances of my Government's intense sympathy and my own, which I venture also to extend at this time of national grief"

### NORWAY

Department of State, October 31, 1912, memorandum:

"The minister of Norway called to inform Mr. Adee of his return to Washington and to express, on his own account and on behalf of his Government, great regret at the death of the Vice President"

From Mr H. H. Bryn, minister of Norway, Washington, to the Secretary of State, October 31, 1912:

"I have the honor to express to the American Government my deepest sympathy on the occasion of the premature death of the Vice President of the United States, whose eminent qualities have won for him the love of his people.

"I also venture to ask your excellency to be good enough to convey to Mrs. Sherman my sincerest condolences."

From Mr H. H. Bryn to the Secretary of State, November 1, 1912:

" I have the honor to acknowledge the receipt of the Hon Alvey A. Adee's note of the 31st ultimo announcing the death at Utica, N. Y., at 9 42 o'clock p. m., on Wednesday, October 30, 1912, of the Hon. JAMES SCHOOLCRAFT SHERMAN, Vice President of the United States.

"According to instructions from my Government, I have the honor to express, through your excellency, to the Government of the United States the Norwegian Government's most sincere sympathy on the painful loss which the country has suffered by the deplorable decease of the Vice President."

### PANAMA

From Belisario Porras, President of Panama, to President Taft:

" PANAMA, *November 1, 1912.*—I send to Your Excellency and to the people of the United States sincere regrets in view of the death of the illustrious Mr SHERMAN "—(Cablegram, translation.)

From Señor Ernesto T. Lefevre, minister for foreign affairs of Panama, to the Secretary of State:

" PANAMA, *November 1, 1912* —In the name of the Government and people of Panama I express to the American Government and people profound sorrow over the death of Vice President SHERMAN "—(Cablegram )

From Señor E T Lefevre, minister for foreign affairs of Panama, to the American chargé d'affaires at Panama, November 2, 1912·

" Through your kind communication No. 265, of yesterday, I have been informed of the sad death of the honorable Vice President of the United States of North America, which occurred on October 31 ultimo.

"In the name of my Government and through your worthy conduct I wish to express to that of the United States my deep sympathy on this mournful incident

"In view of this sad occurrence the proper authority has ordered that on this date the national colors be hoisted to the half-mast in all the public offices.

"Renewing to you the assurances of my high esteem and distinguished consideration, I subscribe myself your kind and obedient servant "

Department of State, October 31, 1912, memorandum:

" The chargé d'affaires of Panama called to-day upon Mr. Adee to express his deep regret at the death of the Vice President."

From Señor Don Juan Brin, chargé d'affaires of Panama, Washington, to the Secretary of State, November 1, 1912:

"With the deepest sorrow I have read the contents of your excellency's obliging note of yesterday, by which you announce the much-lamented death of the Hon JAMES SCHOOLCRAFT SHERMAN, Vice President of the United States, which occurred at Utica, N. Y, at 9.42 p. m. on Wednesday, the 30th of October last, and whose funeral will take place in the same city on Saturday, the 2d instant, at 2 p. m.

"In view of the singular civic virtues and high personal gifts characteristic of the departed statesman and eminent public man, his death is a world-wide, irreparable loss, which all nations must lament, and in the most fitting mourning that now overwhelms the Government and people of this great country, may I be permitted to extend to them, through your excellency's worthy medium, the expressions of sincere sympathy of the Government and people of my country, to which I join my own?"

From Señor Don Juan Brin to the Secretary of State, November 4, 1912:

"I have the honor to transcribe to your excellency the contents of the following cablegram I have just received from my Government, which reads literally as follows:

"'Communicate Department of State the following resolution passed this day by the Assembly:

"'"The National Assembly of Panama, voicing the sentiments of its constituents, sends to the Government and people of the United States of North America the most sincere expression of its condolence on the occasion of the premature death of Mr JAMES S. SHERMAN, Vice President of that friendly Nation."'"

### PERU

From Mr. Federico Alfonso Pezet, minister of Peru, Washington, to the Secretary of State, November 12, 1912:

"I have the honor to acknowledge the receipt of your note, dated October 31, in which you announce the death, at Utica, N. Y, on Wednesday, October 30, of the Hon JAMES SCHOOLCRAFT SHERMAN, Vice President of the United States.

"In reply I have the honor to tender my most sincere condolence on the occasion of a loss so great for the Government and people of the United States"

### PORTUGAL

From President Manoel D Arriaga, of Portugal, to President Taft

"LISBON, *November 2, 1912* —Just now hearing the sad news of the death of the Vice President of the United States of America,

I present to Your Excellency and the friendly Nation the expression of my most sincere condolence."—(Cablegram, translation)

From Viscount de Alte, minister of Portugal, Washington, to the Secretary of State, October 31, 1912:

"I have the honor to acknowledge the receipt of your note of this date announcing the death of the Hon. JAMES SCHOOLCRAFT SHERMAN, Vice President of the United States.

"Painfully impressed by this sad event, I beg that you will, with your usual courtesy, allow me to convey, through you, to the President my heartfelt condolence.

"I also wish to express to you, sir, and to the whole American Government my very great sorrow at the untimely death of Mr. SHERMAN.

"I have been directed by the President and Government of Portugal to express to President Taft and to the American Government their deepest sympathy on the occasion of the great loss the country has sustained through the death of Vice President SHERMAN."

### RUSSIA

Department of State, November 4, 1912, memorandum·

"The Russian ambassador called upon the Acting Secretary of State to-day to say that he was instructed to formally convey the condolences of the Imperial Government upon the lamented death of the Vice President  The ambassador, Mr. Bakhmeteff, said that Russia had followed Mr. SHERMAN's public career with interest and admiration and realized the great loss of the Government of the United States in his death.

"Mr. Adee said that this country and the world at large would mourn the loss of this man whose life had been a great example of kindliness, good fellowship, and always on the side of peace."

### SALVADOR

From President Manuel E. Araujo, of Salvador, to President Taft

"SAN SALVADOR, SALVADOR, *October 31, 1912.*—My Government joins with sympathy in the mourning of the American Government for the death of Vice President SHERMAN."—(Cablegram, translation)

Department of State, October 31, 1912, memorandum:

"The minister of Salvador called upon Mr Adee to-day to express the regret of his Government and his personal sorrow at the death of Vice President SHERMAN.  He will also write an informal note to the department to this effect."

From Señor Don Federico Mejia, minister of Salvador, Washington, to the Secretary of State, November 1, 1912:

"With genuine grief I have read your excellency's valued communication, by which you inform me of the death of the Hon.

JAMES SCHOOLCRAFT SHERMAN, Vice President of the United States of America, and that the funeral will take place in the city of Utica, N. Y., to-morrow at 2 p. m.

"The Salvadorean people profoundly regret the sad event, and I beg your excellency to deign to accept, in the name of my Government and in my own, our most sincere condolences."

From Señor Don Federico Mejia to the Secretary of State, November 1, 1912.

"I am in receipt of special instructions from the Most Excellent the President of Salvador, Dr. Manuel E. Araujo, directing me to express to the Most Excellent Mr. President Taft, through the most worthy medium of your excellency, his sentiments of regrets and profound sorrow for the lamented death of the Hon. JAMES SCHOOLCRAFT SHERMAN, Vice President of the Republic, which has thrown the American people into mourning and deep consternation."

### SERVIA

From Nich. P. Pachitch, ministry of foreign affairs, political section, to the American consul at Belgrade, October 27, 1912:

"I am in receipt of your letter informing me that Mr SHERMAN, the Vice President of the United States, died on October 31, n. s.

"I have the honor to beg you to kindly convey to the United States Government the deepest condolence of the Royal Servian Government."

### SIAM

From the minister for foreign affairs, Devawongse, to the American chargé d'affaires at Bangkok, November 3, 1912:

"I have received with sincerest regret your letter of November 2 announcing the death of the Vice President of the United States of America, Mr. JAMES S SHERMAN, which had taken place on 30th of October last

"I beg to ask that you will be so kind as to convey to the President of the United States of America the deep sympathy of the Siamese Government as well as that of my own."

Department of State, November 1, 1912, memorandum:

"Mr. Loftus, representing the Siamese minister, called to explain that the minister was en route to Europe and would not be able personally to write to the department to express condolence on the death of the Vice President for several weeks. In the meantime, however, Mr. Loftus wished to unofficially transmit the deep sympathy of the Siamese Government"

From Prince Traidos Prabandh, Siamese minister, Washington, to the Secretary of State, November 1, 1912·

"I have the honor to acknowledge the receipt of your letter of the 31st instant, in which you announce the death, at Utica,

N. Y., on Wednesday, October 30 last, of the Hon. James School-craft Sherman, Vice President of the United States.

"In reply, permit me to assure you that His Majesty's Government will deeply regret to learn of the loss which has befallen that of the United States in the passing of this great statesman, and to offer, on their behalf as well as on my own part, an expression of sincere sympathy on this sad occasion."

### SPAIN

From Señor Don Juan Riaño y Gayangos, Spanish minister, Washington, to the Secretary of State, November 1, 1912:

"I have the honor to acknowledge receipt of your excellency's note of yesterday by which you impart to me the sad intelligence of the death at Utica, N. Y., of the Hon. James Schoolcraft Sherman, Vice President of the United States, which occurred on the 30th instant at 9 42 p. m , and that the funeral service will be held at Utica on Saturday, the 2d of November, at 2 p. m.

"In reply, I extend to your excellency my most heartfelt condolence and beg leave to say that I propose to go to Utica to attend the funeral."

### SWEDEN

Department of State, October 31, 1912, memorandum:

"The minister of Sweden called to-day to express his deep regret and that of his Government at the death of the Vice President."

From Mr. W. A. F. Ekengren, minister of Sweden, Washington, to the Secretary of State, November 1, 1912:

"I have had the honor to receive your letter of yesterday with its sorrowful message of the death at Utica, N. Y., on Wednesday last, of the Hon. James Schoolcraft Sherman, Vice President of the United States, and I hasten herewith to repeat the assurance of deep-felt sympathy, which I already have had the occasion to personally express to you, Mr. Secretary, on account of the great loss inflicted not only upon the family of the deceased Vice President but also upon the whole country by the demise of a man so highly beloved as a husband, father, and friend, so highly esteemed as a statesman and legislator

"His memory shall live long amongst them who had the good fortune of his personal acquaintance."

### SWITZERLAND

From Mr Henri Martin, chargé d'affaires of Switzerland, Washington, to the Secretary of State, November 3, 1912:

"I have the honor to acknowledge the receipt of your department's note of October 31 informing me of the death of the Hon

James Schoolcraft Sherman, Vice President of the United States.

"Deeply touched by the unexpected death of Mr. Sherman, I beg you to accept, in behalf of the Swiss Federal Council, the expression of my warm sympathy with the American Nation for the loss of this distinguished statesman."

TURKEY

From Youssouf Zia Pacha, Turkish ambassador, Washington, to the Secretary of State, November 1, 1912:

"I have heard with great regret, by your excellency's note dated October 31 last, of the death of the Hon. James Schoolcraft Sherman, Vice President of the United States of America.

"I beg your excellency kindly to accept the expression of my keenest sympathy on this sorrowful occasion and to receive the assurance of my very high consideration."

URUGUAY

From Dr. Carlos Maria de Pena, minister of Uruguay, Washington, to the Secretary of State, November 1, 1912:

"With profound sorrow have I received your communication announcing the death of the Vice President of the United States and the holding of his obsequies at Utica, November 2, at 2 p. m.

"I beg your excellency to deign to accept and convey to the President the expressions of condolence with which I take part in the mourning of the Nation for the loss of the illustrious Vice President of the United States of America, Mr. James Schoolcraft Sherman.

"In offering this deep sympathy I regret my inability to attend the funeral ceremony."

VENEZUELA

From the ministry of foreign affairs of Venezuela to American chargé d'affaires at Caracas, November 7, 1912·

"With great grief this office has learned, through your honor's courteous note No. 90, of yesterday, that His Excellency Mr. James Schoolcraft Sherman, Vice President of the United States of America, died October 30 last.

"The Government of Venezuela sincerely sympathizes with the friendly nation in its pain over so great a loss and entreats your honor to convey to the Government you so worthily represent an expression of such sympathy."

From Señor Don P. Ezequiel Rojas, minister of Venezuela, Washington, to the Secretary of State, November 1, 1912·

"I have had the honor to receive your obliging letter of yesterday announcing the much-lamented death of the Most Excellent

Mr. James Schoolcraft Sherman, worthy Vice President of the United States, and informing me that the funeral service will be held to-morrow in the city of Utica.

"I deeply deplore the sad event and in the name of my Government tender to the Government of the United States of America, through the Department of State, the most sincere and heartfelt condolence."

### WEST INDIES

From the American consul at Bridgetown, Barbados, West Indies, to the Secretary of State, November 4, 1912·

"On receipt of the telegram on Friday evening (announcing the death of Vice President Sherman) I immediately called up the acting governor of Barbados by telephone and the flags were at half-mast on all Government buildings on Saturday, the day of the funeral, as well as at the various foreign consulates, and the acting governor, Maj. J. A. Burdon, called at the consulate to express his sympathy"

From Mr. Robert Johnstone, colonial secretary, Kingston, Jamaica, to the American vice consul at Kingston, November 2, 1912:

"I am directed by the governor to acknowledge the receipt of your letter of the 1st instant reporting the death of the Hon. James S. Sherman, Vice President of the United States of America. I am to ask you to be so good as to convey to Mr. Bergholz an expression of his excellency's regret on behalf of this Government at the intelligence

"The information as to the death of the Vice President has been immediately communicated by telephone and letter to the deputy assistant adjutant and quartermaster general, for the information of the general officer commanding, and the flags at King's House and Headquarter House will be flown at half-mast to-day as a mark of respect to the deceased"

From the governor of Martinique to the vice consul of the United States at Fort de France, Martinique, November 1, 1912:

"Deeply grieved by the news of the death of Mr. Sherman, Vice President of the Republic of the United States of America, which you have just communicated to me, I wish to express the large share which Martinique takes in the loss of the American Nation and Government of the Republic of the United States

"I beg you to be kind enough to transmit to the American Nation and Government of the Republic the expression of the sentiments of painful sympathy of the colony and of my sincere condolences."

CPSIA information can be obtained at www.ICGtesting.com
Printed in the USA
LVOW02s0420181213

365826LV00005B/132/P